To the Valley Cottage Library

I am honored to share
my childhood wartime memories
with your readers.

Simon Jeruchim

Pomona, November 2001

Hidden in France

Hidden in France

A Boy's Journey
Under the Nazi
Occupation

---

by Simon Jeruchim

FITHIAN PRESS, SANTA BARBARA, CALIFORNIA, 2001

Published by Fithian Press
A division of Daniel and Daniel, Publishers, Inc.
Post Office Box 1525
Santa Barbara, CA 93102
www.danielpublishing.com

LIBRARY OF CONGRESS CATALOGING-IN-PUBLICATION DATA
Jeruchim, Simon, 1929–
Hidden in France : a boy's journey under the Nazi occupation / by Simon
Jeruchim.
    p. cm.
    ISBN 1-56474-360-8 (pbk. : alk. paper)
    1. Jeruchim, Simon, 1929–   . 2. Jewish children in the Holocaust—
France—Biography. 3. Holocaust, Jewish (1939–1945)—France—personal
narratives. 4. Righteous Gentiles in the Holocaust—France—Biography. 5.
France—Biography. I. Title.
    DS135.F9 J475 2001
    940.53'18'0830944—dc21
                            00-0011262

To the memory of my mother, Sonia,
and my father, Samuel,

.

to my sister, Alice, and to my brother, Michel,
who shared my journey,

.

and to my children and grandchildren
and future generations

so that they will never forget.

Acknowledgments

I wish to express my gratitude to friends who have been of special help in my undertaking: to Jerry Steinman, who early on showed a great deal of interest in my project and gave me useful hints on how to shape my story; to Dick Elfenbein, who generously gave his time to read through a late draft and provided helpful criticism and editing.

To my family I extend my warmest thanks and hugs: to my daughter Aviva, who enthusiastically gave me thumbs up and contributed some insightful editing; to my other daughter, Linda, whose positive response to my story meant a great deal to me; to my sister, Alice, who was quite helpful in sharing her memories of our childhood and of some wartime events. Alice also had the presence of mind to tape a conversation with our Uncle David during one of his visits to New York, thus providing additional recollections of earlier times in Poland and of our parents.

Above all, I am deeply grateful to my wife, Cécile, who was there for me from the very beginning to the end of writing my memoir. Herself a hidden child and a Holocaust survivor, Cécile was able to fully appreciate the difficult task I undertook. She kept encouraging me with her suggestions, moral support and her love.

Contents

Preface

Many years have passed since I was in France during the Nazi occupation, yet most of my memories of this harrowing period of my life have remained vividly alive. In the spring of 1991 my past was dramatically evoked at an international conference I attended in New York City for Jewish survivors of the Holocaust who, like me, were hidden children during World War II. This gathering, aptly named "The Hidden Child," gave us an opportunity to try to deal with repressed emotions of our collective past, and to understand that, as survivors, we had an obligation to bear witness to the events of the war for our children and future generations.

Prior to this conference it never occurred to me that the story of my past should be told. And yet it was evident that survivors like myself represented the last generation who lived through the Holocaust and could still testify about their individual plight and suffering. This new awareness helped me find the courage and determination to give voice to the boy hidden in France during the war.

In the course of examining the past I was reminded of the shameful conduct of the French government toward its Jewish population during the occupation and also of the inordinate number of Frenchmen who collaborated with the Nazis in denouncing their Jewish neighbors.

Nonetheless there were accounts of a handful of courageous French people, gentiles, who selflessly rescued Jews from the clutches of the Gestapo and the French police. During those dark days my family had the good fortune to meet such strangers who came to help us and in the process took enormous personal risks.

My sister, my brother and I survived the horrors of the war, but my parents could not be saved. They were murdered by the Nazis. My mother was forty-two years old, my father forty-four.

11

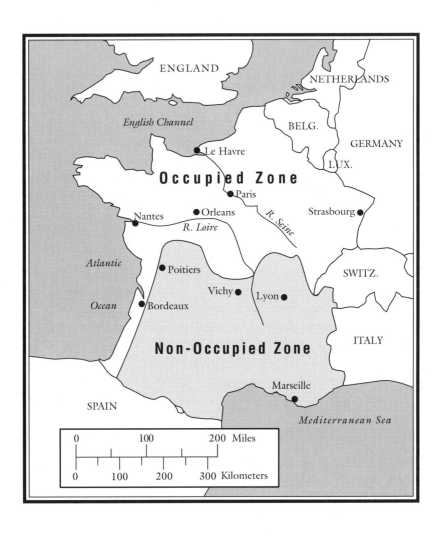

ENGLAND

NETHERLANDS

English Channel

BELG.

GERMANY

LUX.

Le Havre

Occupied Zone

Paris

Nantes

Orleans

R. Loire

R. Seine

Strasbourg

Atlantic

Poitiers

SWITZ.

Vichy

Lyon

Ocean

Bordeaux

ITALY

Non-Occupied Zone

Marseille

SPAIN

Mediterranean Sea

```
0          100          200  Miles
|----|----|----|----|----|
0         100    200    300  Kilometers
```

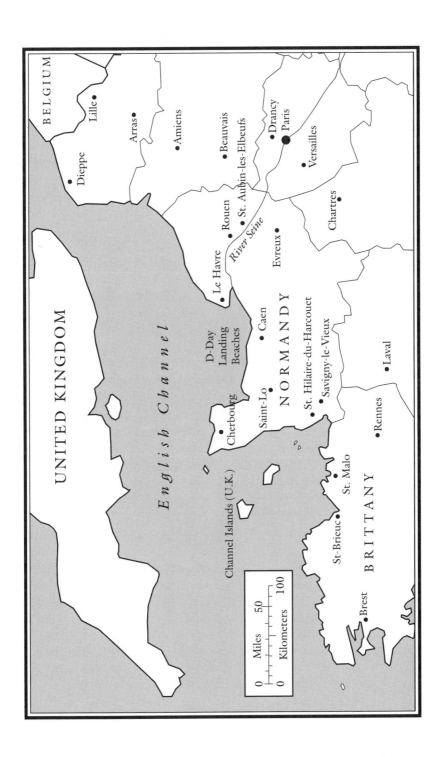

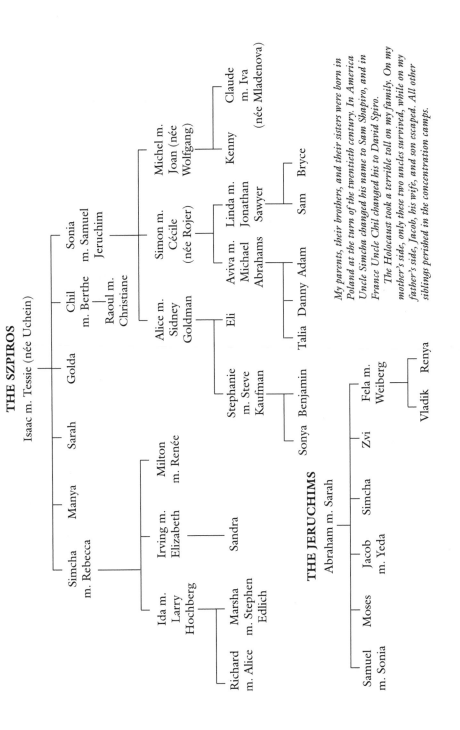

THE SZPIROS

Isaac m. Tessie (née Uchein)

Simcha m. Rebecca

Manya

Sarah

Golda

Chil m. Berthe
Raoul m. Christiane

Sonia m. Samuel Jeruchim

Ida m. Larry Hochberg

Irving m. Elizabeth

Milton m. Renée

Alice m. Sidney Goldman

Simon m. Cécile (née Rojer)

Michel m. Joan (née Wolfgang)

Richard m. Alice

Marsha m. Stephen Edlich

Sandra

Stephanie m. Steve Kaufman

Eli

Aviva m. Michael Abrahams

Linda m. Jonathan Sawyer

Kenny

Claude m. Iva (née Mladenova)

Sonya

Benjamin

Talia

Danny

Adam

Sam

Bryce

THE JERUCHIMS

Abraham m. Sarah

Moses

Jacob m. Yeda

Simcha

Zvi

Fela m. Weiberg

Samuel m. Sonia

Vladik

Renya

My parents, their brothers, and their sisters were born in Poland at the turn of the twentieth century. In America Uncle Simcha changed his name to Sam Shapiro, and in France Uncle Chil changed his to David Spiro.

The Holocaust took a terrible toll on my family. On my mother's side, only these two uncles survived, while on my father's side, Jacob, his wife, and son escaped. All other siblings perished in the concentration camps.

Hidden in France

Introduction

Montreuil, Fall 1983
I have few mementos left from my childhood and only one precious sepia photograph of me with my family when I was seven years old. The war swept away all of our possessions. I emigrated from France to America in 1949, when I was nineteen. Decades later, as a grown man, I returned with my wife, Cécile, on a sentimental journey to my old neighborhood.

From Paris we traveled by metro to the eastern suburb of Montreuil. The bright October sunshine greeted us as we made our way along the narrow cobblestone streets. Was this the neighborhood where I used to live? Time was playing tricks on my memory, but as we got closer to my house the landmarks became familiar again. Images of my past surged, of happy times, but also of terror when overnight the Nazi occupation transformed my neighborhood into a hostile and dangerous place.

We arrived at my old apartment house located in Rue Colmet-Lepinay at the corner of Boulevard Jeanne d'Arc. The six-story gray brick-and-stone building with wrought-iron balconies was in surprisingly good repair despite decades of weathering. I was anxious to have another look at my apartment. I pressed the buzzer, and a curtain parted on the ground floor window while darting eyes examined the intruders. In the small lobby we were met by the concierge, a heavyset, grumpy woman wearing a kerchief on her head.

She snapped, "Who are you looking for?" I managed to ignore her suspicious gaze and went on to explain the purpose of our visit. She was not mollified by my story until I made a passing comment about the concierge who had worked in the building during the war, a woman by the name of Mrs. Ackerman. Her surly expression gave way instantly to a broad smile. *"Ca alors!"* (I'll be darned!) she exclaimed. She told me that Mrs. Ackerman was still one of her tenants.

The concierge warned me that old age had clouded Mrs. Ackerman's memory, but that she would be happy to take us to her apartment. An old and frail woman clutching a shawl around her shoulders opened the door. Old age had left its toll on the once quite attractive and energetic woman, who was now stooped and withered. The younger concierge cupped one hand around her mouth and shouted to Mrs. Ackerman, *"Vous avez de la visite, des Americains!"* (You have company, Americans!)

Mrs. Ackerman was understandably at a loss until I remembered to tell her I was *"le petit Zizi"* (little Zizi). Zizi was my nickname as a young boy. A flicker of recognition sparked her watery eyes, and reaching out for me with a wrinkled hand she excitedly pulled me inside. We sat in her living room and talked for a while about the past and of course about my parents. I was grateful that she remembered them as well as she did.

She reflected, "Your mother was a kind woman, always ready to do me a favor—and your father was also a very nice man, ever so polite."

After I alluded to the police roundup of 1942 she became pensive and lashed out angrily, "The police and *les Boches* (the Krauts), they were all monsters!"

Mrs. Ackerman got up from her armchair and rummaged through a stack of books and magazines until she retrieved a photo album. She pulled out several photographs of herself as a young woman with a smiling little girl. She pointed to the pretty child, murmuring, "My daughter was so young when she died." She began sobbing quietly, pressing the photographs tightly against her chest.

The heavy velvet drapes drawn across the window kept the dimly lit living room in a mournful grip, shutting out the bright October sun. My eyes roamed around the crowded furnishings. I gazed one by one at the mementos of a lifetime that were heaped on a dresser and at photographs and pictures displayed along one of the walls. A small still-life with flowers in delicate shades of pink and blue stood out among the faded sepia photographs.

I kept thinking that there was something oddly familiar about this oil painting, and then it came back to me. I remembered that it had been purchased by my mother and hung in our dining room next to the window. I had not seen this painting since the summer of 1942, when we fled our apartment in order to save our lives.

In my excitement I was about to blurt out what I had just discovered. But on second thought I realized that anything I might say to Mrs. Ackerman would imply that the painting was not hers or, even worse, that she had appropriated it. I didn't have the heart to upset her and kept my lips sealed.

Mrs. Ackerman looked tired, confused. She was mixing up events and people she had known, gazing in the distance as though ghosts of her past were parading in front of her.

We finally took leave of the old concierge and were relieved to escape from the dark living room filled with sad memories.

We went up to my former apartment on the second floor, climbing along the same wooden steps that had been my pathway to the outside world. A wary-looking woman wearing an apron cautiously opened the door. Smells of cooking drifted out. Through the narrow opening I glimpsed the hallway where I often played with my younger brother, Michel. For an instant I replayed a familiar scene in my mind. The two of us were squatting at either end of the hallway, noisily pushing one of my brother's favorite toys, a metal milk-wagon filled with tin bottles, back and forth. My mother's voice rang out of the kitchen, screaming at me for behaving like a child.

The woman's inquisitive gaze quickly brought me back to earth. While I explained to her that I was hoping to have another look at the place where I grew up, she remained unmoved, holding on to the doorknob and barring the way, as though I was about to push my way inside her apartment. "I can't let you in. I am too busy right now," she snapped, slamming the door in our faces as she retreated inside.

Our next stop was a short walk to Rue Diderot in Vincennes, another suburban neighborhood, where I lived until the age of eight. Back then the street had many small stores where we did most of our food shopping. I was glad to see that some stores had remained almost the way I remembered them. We walked by the bakery. An aroma of freshly baked bread reminded me of my daily errands, when my mother sent me there to buy crusty baguettes.

The café-tabac was still the busy social hub it had been when my father bought cigarettes and his weekly lottery ticket there. Up the block the tiny candy store once more beckoned me inside, where once a week I had run to buy the Mickey comics for a couple of sous. Unfortunately the hardware store, which had rivaled the candy store as my favorite place, was no longer there.

As a favor to my parents Mr. Lefèvre, the owner of the hardware and paint store across the street from where we had lived, allowed me to browse around the aisles to my heart's content as long as I didn't touch anything and kept out of the way of customers. The store was like my private museum. Even at a young age I was attracted by shapes and colors, intrigued by forms and fascinated by logos on storefronts and posters in the metro. I vowed that as a grown-up I would be an artist, although at times I wavered in my commitment, thinking that being a train engineer would also be quite thrilling.

I have never forgotten the excitement I felt when Mr. Lefèvre gave me a paint-color chart, which I safely kept tucked inside my school notebook like a special talisman. Even the names of the color swatches were beautiful, with evocative descriptions like "golden yellow," "horizon blue," "ivory white," "sage green," "royal blue," "Chinese red" and so many others I tried to memorize.

The butcher shop was gone, and with it the golden horse head that had adorned the storefront. After school I often played with the butcher's son. His name was Marcel. He was about my age, a jovial, even-tempered boy with a thatch of red hair. I was devastated when he suddenly died of a brain tumor. It was the first time I became aware of my own mortality.

My wife and I arrived at the apartment house where I had lived, which still stood tall in the middle of the block. We walked to the back of the building and into a cobblestone courtyard where I had often played tag with my friends after school. I stood there for a while, looking up at the small rear windows and trying to locate the one where my mother had often leaned over the ledge to summon me for supper.

It was getting late. We walked back to the metro. I turned around for a last glance at my old neighborhood. The cavalcade of past images was already fading in the early twilight.

France at War

1

Richebourg, September 3, 1939

It began as an ordinary day, another fun day in the country. I was nine years old. It was the last week of my summer vacation with my parents, my older sister Alice, my baby brother Michel, and our close friends, Mr. and Mrs. Krum and their son Joseph.

Richebourg was a quiet little village nestled in the western countryside of Normandy, about one hour by train from Paris. We had come back to the same place for many summers, and my parents always rented several rooms in the house of Mrs. Balossier for us and for their friends. We had the run of her rambling old house, and she didn't seem to mind our noisy company. Mrs. Balossier was a kind woman with a jolly laugh who spoiled us with her tasty cooking and delicious fruit pies.

However, on this pleasant late-summer day we had no inkling that our lives would be drastically changed by a news report. Alice, Joseph and I were sent to a nearby farm for milk and eggs. When we came back from our errand we found my parents and their friends in the kitchen looking quite dejected. Mrs. Balossier told us in a shaky voice that they had just heard on the radio that France and England had declared war against Germany.

Suddenly war loomed real and terribly frightening. Up to that moment my perception of war had been about battles waged a long time ago, the ones I'd read about in my history book. Even World War I, prematurely described as "the war to end all wars," was for me just another distant chapter in the long story of human conflict. I didn't pay any attention to the early reports of the war, even after my father had told me the year before that Nazi Germany had annexed Austria and invaded Czechoslovakia. I was too young then to appreciate the importance of such news. At that time those events didn't seem like they could have an impact upon our lives in France. Not until Hitler threatened to invade Poland had the unthinkable taken place—France was at war!

My parents were having a lively discussion with Mr. and Mrs. Krum. They spoke mostly in Yiddish, with an occasional sprinkling of French words. I only knew a smattering of Yiddish, mostly expressions, but not enough to follow their conversation. Nonetheless I gathered that the topic was Germany because Hitler's name was mentioned repeatedly. My parents and their close circle of friends were Jewish immigrants from Poland; while they could manage to speak French, Yiddish or sometime even Polish were their languages of choice when they got together.

When it was time to leave my parents decided to keep Alice and me in Richebourg for a while longer because of reported German threats to bomb large cities. Mrs. Balossier agreed to look after us until my parents felt that it was safe for us to come back home. I was worried about my parents and my brother, wondering if they would be in danger in Montreuil. But I also realized that my father had to go back home to work and that my mother had to remain by his side with my little brother. It was a tearful goodbye. I was lucky that my sister stayed with me. We were quite inseparable, and with Alice I felt protected and less lonesome while we were separated from our parents.

Alice and I were enrolled at the village school, where we met our new teachers, Mr. and Mrs. Lacroix. They were a young, outgoing couple who immediately made us feel welcome. Unlike our schools in Montreuil, where boys and girls were in separate classes, in Richebourg my sister and I sat together in a one-room schoolhouse.

As we were unfamiliar Parisians, our arrival was greeted with curious stares from the other children. As such, we were accorded a special status, as though being from Paris automatically made us smarter. Actually, Alice and I quickly discovered that scholastically we were indeed ahead of our schoolmates, but on the other hand they surpassed us in their knowledge of botany and gardening.

New horizons opened for us when we went with Mr. Lacroix on long nature walks around the countryside. I took notes and made little drawings of the trees he named along the way. After a while I was able to identify trees by the textures and colors of their bark and by the shapes of their leaves. When I wasn't in class I also helped out in the vegetable garden behind the school, learning how to use a rake and a spade.

Richebourg, late September 1939

"Poland Surrenders to Germany!" screamed the newspaper headline. Incredibly, less than three weeks after the war started, German tanks and bombers had crushed Poland and left Warsaw in ruins. Mrs. Balossier, rarely angry, was seething when she read the news. She summed up the political situation for us, "I wish somebody would tell me how Hitler can thumb his nose at us and get away with it!" referring of course to France and England's inability to prevent or stop Nazi Germany's aggression against Poland.

Richebourg, October 1939

Mr. Lacroix pinned small French flags on a map along the Franco-German border in order to show us where the famous Maginot Line was located. He said the Maginot Line was a concrete fortress-like wall extending for hundreds of miles along the German border, with guns pointing toward the enemy and manned day and night by our soldiers at the ready. "The Germans will never be able to invade our country like they did in 1914," he asserted. His confident words put to rest our fears that our country might suffer the terrible fate of Poland.

Our teacher's patriotic spirit was so contagious that all of us wanted to help with the war effort. Mr. Lacroix suggested that by writing letters to the men on the frontline we would be doing our part. "Let's express our thanks for their courage, *mes enfants!*" he declared. We were all filled with pride, imagining soldiers taking pleasure in reading our letters. I even inserted a couple of funny drawings in my letter hoping to cheer up the unknown recipient. For her part, Mrs. Lacroix taught the girls how to knit ski hats and scarves to keep the soldiers warm.

One day Mr. Lacroix said that instead of our regular class he would show us a movie to reward us for our fine patriotic conduct.

Since the closest movie house was miles away in the next town, it was a special treat for everyone. Alice and I were probably not as deprived as the village kids, yet we were also thrilled by such an unexpected diversion.

We promptly closed all the shutters and hung a bed sheet against a wall, and Mr. Lacroix cranked up his antique projector in the darkened classroom. After several false starts, the movie title, *The Count of Monte Cristo*, finally flashed on the small screen and was greeted by a collective sigh of relief. As the swashbuckling epic unfolded, not a sound could be heard except the clickety-click of the projector.

Although the black-and-white film was quite old and grainy, we were all glued to the screen in perfect communion.

Richebourg, November 1939

There were already sure signs that winter was coming. The morning frost created shimmering crystal patterns upon the faded summer flowers, and sparrows noisily perched on overhead wires, ready to fly off to warmer climes.

Mrs. Balossier's house, like most houses in rural areas, had no central heating, and at night the bedrooms were ice cold. Fortunately the thick blanket filled with goose feathers provided by Mrs. Balossier kept me comfortably warm, as did the hot water bottle I kept against my feet.

Since the beginning of the war there had been such a scarcity of news that at times it looked as though the whole thing had never happened. However, the sudden arrival of a British convoy in Richebourg not only caused quite a stir, but dispelled any notion that the war was over. It was probably the first time ever that a contingent of soldiers had come to Richebourg. Upon hearing the news, people came at once in droves to the village's main square to greet our allies, whom we nicknamed "Tommies." By the time Mrs. Balossier, Alice and I made our way there, dozens of military trucks and other types of armored vehicles were already parked all along the curb. We wove through the crowd to get a closer look at the young-looking men in khaki uniforms sitting outside the local café. They were drinking, laughing and flirting with the waitresses as though they didn't have a care in the world.

For the next couple of days the Tommies bivouacked in a pasture near the village, but soon their tents were down and the British were preparing to leave. Mr. Lacroix dismissed our class to see them off. We went over to the campgrounds, joining a crowd of cheering villagers waving homemade British flags. As the convoy noisily rolled by, we took a last look at the soldiers' smiling faces. Soon the last truck had vanished at the bend of the dirt road. I couldn't help but wonder how many Tommies would return home from the war.

Richebourg, December 24, 1939

We were going home! I didn't have the heart to jump for joy, for I saw Mrs. Balossier looking quite distressed after reading that my father was coming to take us back to Montreuil. When the much anticipated day arrived, I posted myself in the front parlor of the house, patiently watching through the window for my father's appearance. I wanted to be the first one to open the door for him. From a distance I recognized at once his distinctive tall silhouette and long strides as he came toward the house carrying a small suitcase. There could be no mistaking my dad with his beret and raincoat that he often wore. Minutes later Alice and I were in our father's safe embrace, cuddling next to him, enjoying the soothing warmth of his hands around our shoulders. My father brought presents for Mrs. Balossier to thank her for looking after us, and also for Mr. and Mrs. Lacroix. Alice and I were excited to go home but also felt a twinge of sadness to be leaving Mrs. Balossier, who had been so caring toward us. We promised to write and to see her again on our next summer vacation.

We left on Christmas Eve, just one day before my tenth birthday. In Paris, the Montparnasse railroad station was crowded with holiday travelers and soldiers, a reminder that we were still at war. On the metro back to Montreuil I was thrilled by the new crop of colorful posters in every station along the way.

Rue Colmet-Lepinay at last! My heart was beating faster. Our concierge, Mrs. Ackerman, greeted us warmly and made a big fuss at how Alice and I had such nice red cheeks and how much we had grown since the beginning of the summer.

Alice and I rushed up the flight of steps. My mother and Michel appeared in the doorway. My brother let go of my mother's dress and shyly ran up to us to give us each a kiss. My mother's large brown eyes were filled with tears of joy. I rushed into her arms, feeling wonderfully safe and happy in her embrace.

It was so wonderful to be back home. The familiar smell of freshly waxed wood floors reminded me to use felt pads to walk around, in order to help my mother keep the floors clean and shinny. I was gliding from one room to another, surveying our apartment, making a visual inventory of the rooms and looking for any changes. But I was happy to find that everything seemed to have remained the same since I'd left, including my collection of adventure books, still neatly stacked in the bookcase above the studio bed I was sharing with my sister.

I almost walked by without noticing a gift-wrapped package with my name on it, squeezed between two books. My parents had cleverly hidden my birthday present there. Not entirely unexpected, it was *White Fang*, one of the adventure books I had wished for.

Montreuil, January 1940

I felt extremely fortunate that I had been born in France rather than Poland. When my parents spoke about their past in their native country, they often alluded to anti-Semitic repressions and pogroms. Because of their stories I visualized Poland only as a bleak and hostile place. Yet most of their brothers and sisters lived there. I knew that my parents were born at the turn of the twentieth century in Poland, in small towns near Warsaw, my father in Ostrow and my mother in Garwolin. Their given names were Samuel and Sonia, and they both came from large families. My father had four brothers and one sister and my mother had two brothers and three sisters.

My relationship with my parents' families was very limited. My maternal grandmother resided in New York with her eldest son. I recalled meeting her once when she came on a brief visit to France. Although my mother's other brother also lived in France, we never saw him because of a quarrel with my mother.

I questioned my parents as to why they settled in France when the majority of their siblings had remained in Poland. My father explained that emigrating was not a simple matter. There were so many obstacles in the way that most people eventually gave up. Not only were money, passports and visas needed, a sponsor had to get the necessary permits in order for an emigrant to become a permanent resident.

My father said that during the 1920s he had been offered a job by Mr. Eichenbaum, an acquaintance from Poland who had settled near Paris and had built a lucrative business repairing and selling new watches just a couple of years earlier.

When it became necessary for Mr. Eichenbaum to hire some additional help for his growing business, he remembered my father's reputation as a reliable and skilled watchmaker. After settling in his job and saving some money, my father was able to send for my mother. Soon after she arrived, they were married in Vincennes in the home of the Eichenbaums.

Emigrating to France was one of my father's fondest dreams come true. He often said that, "France was a beacon of freedom and equality." He admitted that his perspective had been shaped by books he'd read in translation by French authors like Victor Hugo and Emile Zola, whose writings appealed to his socialist ideals.

Montreuil, February 1940

It had been about six months since the war started, and the news about the fighting was uneventful. "The War Is at a Standstill!" shouted the banner headline in "Le Populaire," my father's favorite newspaper, which he read religiously every day. But overnight our complacency was shattered by rumors of German airplanes bombing some French border cities.

Perhaps those rumors were true, for we began having weekly air-raid drills at my school. At the shrill sound of the school bell, we all ran in single file, led by our teacher, Mr. Delaunay, down to the basement, where we remained until the "all-clear" signal was given. Such drills were always opportunities for some kids to clown around and make catcalls, to the despair of Mr. Delaunay, who tried in vain to restore some order.

We became more aware of the threat of air raids when Montreuil declared a total blackout. Air-raid wardens patrolled our neighborhood at night to enforce the ordinance. At times, when we heard whistles warning people that light was showing, we automatically ran to our windows facing the street, making sure that our drapes were tightly drawn together.

During air-raid alerts we had to take shelter in our apartment house basement. It seemed uncanny that most alerts occurred in the middle of the night. The shrill wailing of sirens jolted us from our deep sleep. We dressed in a hurry and ran downstairs. All at once the sound of slamming doors and rapid footsteps echoed up and down the stairwell.

We joined other sleepy neighbors carrying flashlights and flickering candles in the basement, a long tunnel-like hallway with a dirt floor. Doors on both sides of the hallway accessed storage cubicles. Only one bare bulb cast a gloomy halo over our weary gathering. Some people were still wearing pajamas and nightgowns with blankets draped over their shoulders; others had coats on, and some even wore scarves and hats to ward off the cold. A couple of benches were brought into the basement for women with young children and elderly people to sit down during lengthy alerts. Thus my mother had a chance to rest while cradling my sleepy little brother on her lap.

Time seemed suspended in such gloomy surroundings, minutes passed slowly while we waited for those alerts to end. My father chatted with Mr. Gronner, an acquaintance from the second floor with whom my father played an occasional chess game. Alice and I played word games to stay awake and to keep our minds off our fear that one day bombs would really fall on our building. People whispered, as though the sound of their voices could possibly make our presence known to German pilots. Eventually the sirens sounded the "all-clear" signal; then everyone warily and silently filed out of the basement, shuffling back upstairs to bed.

Montreuil, March 1940

I came home one day from school with an army-issue khaki metal canister dangling from my shoulder. My mother and brother were dying of curiosity, but before they had a chance to question me, I ran in the next room and strapped on the gas mask I'd just received from my teacher. I quickly returned and made a grand entrance, enjoying the surprise painted on their faces. Michel then shrieked in mock terror, and my mother broke out in laughter. When I spotted my reflection in a mirror, I was able to appreciate the full effect I'd made upon them. I looked like a comical monster with large, glassy round eyes and a long rubber snout protruding from my face.

After we all had a good laugh, I told my mother that my teacher had instructed us to carry our gas masks at all times. Mr. Delaunay said that during World War I the Germans had used deadly gas against our troops, and warned us that another attack was possible. "Even innocent civilians could be targeted and die horrible deaths!" he had declared. We had periodic drills in school, during which we quickly strapped on our gas masks and kept them on for short periods of time. We dreaded the drills because even minutes spent in the confinement of clammy rubber made our breathing quite difficult. We anxiously waited for Mr. Delaunay, looking at his pocket watch, to wave his hand and signal that the test was over.

Montreuil, April 1940
Depressing news of the war trickled in, mostly about Nazi Germany invading smaller and weaker nations. Denmark had just surrendered and Norway was under attack by German forces.

Montreuil, May 1940
We heard that Luxembourg and the Netherlands had surrendered and that Belgium was now under attack by German bombers and armored units. Two weeks later the war took a turn for the worse when, despite a valiant counterattack, Belgium was overwhelmed by the powerful German armies and had to lay down their arms.

Adding to those fast-moving events, it was reported that German troops had launched an offensive against our own forces.

As if this discouraging news were not enough to cause consternation, my parents were informed that all school children would be evacuated at once to the country south of Paris, in the vicinity of Orleans. The local authorities met with parents to explain that the evacuation was only a preventive measure, and that all children would be back as soon as the threat of an invasion had subsided.

Within days Alice and I reported in front of the Montreuil city hall with a knapsack and a change of clothing. The square was filled with anxious parents and clinging children. My parents tried their best to comfort us, but their faces betrayed their own apprehension. A long line of buses stretched along the curb. Alice and I said good-bye as she boarded a bus with her class. I was saddened that we would be separated and shipped to different locations. When it was my turn to join my class, my mother furtively pressed into my hand a handful of sous.

She whispered, "Treat yourself to a comic book." She didn't want my father to find out I was going to spend good money on what he described as *"du gaspillage"* (a waste). It was my father's favorite expression denoting anything that was not constructive. From the bus I waved a last goodbye to my parents and to my brother, managing to hide my tears and put a brave face on for their benefit, but also not wanting to give the tough boys in my class an opportunity to call me a sissy.

2

Château de la Barre, June 1940

We traveled for hours along narrow two-lane country roads, occasionally coming to a stop when a herd of cows or a flock of sheep blocked our way. The flat countryside stretched to the horizon. It was a monotonous landscape of pastures and fields dotted with small farms and villages. We arrived at our destination, named Château de la Barre, a sprawling baronial manor with steep slate roofs and massive chimneys.

We had supper in a cavernous room decorated with hunting trophies. The hearty meal was prepared and served by local farmers who did their best to keep up with our hunger. At night we were assigned to dormitories, sleeping on cots in large rooms emptied of their contents, except for tapestries and paintings still left hanging on tall paneled walls.

The next morning we were assembled in the courtyard. The head counselor told us what he expected from us, with a stern warming that if we didn't follow the rules we would be punished. We were split in teams and assigned chores. We took turns sweeping the dining room, setting up and clearing tables and washing dishes.

Other than the assigned chores, we were free to play. Soccer was by far our most popular pastime, but since not everyone could get into a game it led to fights. Several weeks went by without letters or news. We were not allowed outside the grounds, and at times we felt like prisoners.

I was told to report at once to the head counselor's office. I was nervous and wondered if I had committed some infraction of the rules. I rushed over and, to my astonishment, I found my father with the head counselor. I thought I was dreaming until my father hugged me so hard it hurt. I was too excited to ask him why he had come, until we found a quiet place outside where we could talk.

My father told me of the events that had brought him to the château. He said that shortly after Alice and I left the sudden news of the French army's retreat spread instant panic in the population. People still remembered World War I and the atrocities committed by German soldiers against civilians. Anyone with relatives or friends in southern France left Paris to escape from the threat of advancing German troops. At the last minute my mother remembered that her good friend in Vincennes, Mrs. Lefèvre, had an aunt in the southwest. Through Mrs. Lefèvre my parents contacted Mrs. Saulnier, who agreed to take us in. My parents left Montreuil on a crowded train bound for Orleans, the closest town to the places where Alice and I were staying.

While my mother and Michel remained in a hotel in town, my father had planned to get Alice and me back to Orleans as soon as possible and to have all of us travel on to the village of St. Savinien, where Mrs. Saulnier lived. Unfortunately his plans went awry when, to his dismay, he quickly found out that no transportation was available. My father's only option was to walk the long fifteen miles to the Château de la Barre. I felt so proud of my father's grit and determination. He paused to light up a cigarette, looking exhausted but happy he'd found me.

The next morning we left for the long walk to the village of Coulmiers, where my sister was staying. At the beginning I eagerly trotted by my father's side to keep up with his long strides. However, after a couple of miles at such a fast pace I felt my resolve wilting, but I was unwilling to tell my father that I was tired. The dirt road meandered through the flat countryside with hardly a soul in sight, except for an occasional farmer riding a horse-drawn wagon, or a lone bicyclist. We came upon a sleepy village and stopped to cool off at a public pump and to munch on sandwiches we'd taken along.

We resumed walking without shade to protect us from the noon sun. Suddenly my sagging spirits soared when I spied a tantalizing grove of trees in the distance and what appeared to be military trucks parked next to it along the road. "What if we are lucky enough to get a ride?" I excitedly asked my father. Not wanting to dash my hopes he took a wait-and-see attitude. It turned out to be a British military convoy parked in the shade with soldiers taking a break, sitting in the grass and smoking. My father approached an officer who, despite his obvious lack of French, was able to understand sign language. The officer must have felt sorry for us because of our weary appearance for he nodded his approval. He signaled one of his men to lead us to a truck. My father and I sat between burly soldiers, thrilled by such a break.

We departed, the convoy leaving behind a wake of white swirling dust. The miles quickly vanished. Soon a road sign indicated Coulmiers. We left the friendly Tommies with profuse thanks, grateful for their kindness. With some villagers' help we found the Château of Coulmiers, where my sister was staying. Alice was shocked to see us, reacting in much the same way that I had the day before. After our emotional reunion my father cleared up the mystery of our sudden presence and brought her up to date. We were allowed to stay overnight at the château. The next morning we went to the village hoping to find a ride back to Orleans. Alas, there was no transportation available. Twenty-five miles seemed just too far to manage on foot with our knapsacks on our backs and the small suitcase my father was lugging along.

At the local café someone suggested that we try the bicycle store where we might find some used bikes. My father thought it was an idea worth a try as a last resort. The store owner pointed to a pile of rusty bikes in the back room. He readily admitted that they didn't inspire confidence, but insisted that once he put air in the tires and oiled the gears and chains they would be as good as new. We couldn't afford to be choosy. My father went on to select three bikes, but even the best looking ones of the lot were in a sorry state, with bald tires and no working brakes. My father struck a bargain with the store owner, who looked happy to get rid of the old wrecks for a handful of francs. My father tied his suitcase behind his bicycle seat with a rope, hoping the makeshift arrangement would hold until we reached Orleans. We practiced braking by using the soles of our shoes on the front tires. It was at best a precarious way to slow down, but it was our only option. We went on our way, hoping our bikes wouldn't let us down.

On the way to Orleans, June 1940
We moved at a good pace and, surprisingly, our bikes held up. My
father estimated that we had traveled more than halfway to Orleans.
It boded well for the rest of our trip. The countryside around us was
similar to what we had seen the day before, quiet, with only the
summer sounds of insects breaking up the silence. The road was
practically deserted until we reached the main highway going south-
east to Orleans. We came upon a noisy human tidal wave stretching
as far as we could see, clogged with refugees of every age. Some people walked with bundles on their backs, others rode bicycles, pulling
makeshift trailers loaded with suitcases and children. Still others
were pushing handcarts filled with their meager belongings.

The more fortunate refugees rode in battered trucks, old cars
and horse-wagons piled high with an odd assortment of home furnishings, from chairs to mattresses and even grandfather clocks. We
had no choice but to join this unending, mad parade. I wondered
where all these people were going, as everyone doggedly kept moving forward, united by the fear of the German invaders. A road sign
read, "Orleans–10 kms." Only six miles away. The thought that my
father, my sister and I would soon be able to leave this crowd and re-
join my mother and my brother buoyed my flagging spirits.

However, my hopes were dashed when a couple of miles farther,
at an intersection, we ran into French soldiers blocking the highway.
They were standing in front of barricades and waving everybody off
the highway to the other road. It was so heartbreaking to be turned
away, being so close to our goal! We heard that the town of Orleans
had been bombed by the Germans the night before and was closed
to civilians. I was haunted by a vision of my mother and brother
dead and buried under a pile of rubble. I broke into tears. My father
managed to calm me down. As usual his composure and optimism
won me over, instilling confidence in me that they were safe and that
my mother would find a way to meet us in St. Savinien.

We followed the country road to Châteauneuf-sur-Loire, a town on
the edge of the river. There we hoped to find a bridge that the Germans had not yet destroyed. At last the steep roofs and church tow-
ers of the town emerged beyond wheat fields gleaming in the

sunlight. The ominous roar of airplanes caught us by surprise. My heart skipped a beat when I saw dozens of German aircraft above Châteauneuf-sur-Loire. Soon thundering explosions rocked the countryside, instantly followed by bursts of red and orange flames and columns of black smoke rising over the town.

The German airplanes soon disappeared behind a widening screen of smoke rising into the sky. The attack came so unexpectedly and so swiftly that we just stood there mesmerized by the bombing. Some people panicked and scattered through the fields, but it was obvious that no one could hide in the flat, open countryside. All of us were targets for the enemy. After some moments of indecision, the rest of us kept marching forward. Alice and I were quite shaken by this incident. My father tried reassuring us that we had little to fear. He believed the Germans were only after military targets and would not waste bombs on civilians. As much as I wanted to believe my father, my fertile imagination was unrelenting. I visualized the bombers attacking us and imagined the ensuing carnage, a scene of dead bodies littering the road.

When we arrived in Châteauneuf-sur-Loire the smoke had dissipated, but the acrid smell of charred timber lingered on. Collapsed houses were still smoldering, and French soldiers had set up roadblocks, keeping people from entering the town. We were diverted to another road, which led to the Loire River. There were cries of excitement when a bridge with massive arches came into view, still intact, having so far escaped destruction. We somehow made our way across the bridge, fearing that we would be trampled by horses and wagons crowding the narrow roadway, more than the threat of German bombers. Making it safely to the other side seemed like a good omen for the rest of our trip.

On the road to St. Savinien, June 1940

The next couple of weeks were free from danger, but the days were long and tiring as we followed the crowd of refugees marching south. Fortunately for us not everybody had fled their homes and farms. Many farmers chose to stay to look after their lands and cattle and were willing to sell us food, but at a steep price.

We did not eat well, but we never starved. Some milk, a loaf of bread and cheese quickly filled our bellies. We slept in barns in the company of other refugees. I was so weary at night that even a hard bed of straw was welcomed. All of us were grimy-looking, managing to wash only when we found a well or a stream.

Even though we knew the German forces were already on French soil, we were shocked to hear that columns of Panzer tanks were near Paris.

Day after day we kept moving farther south, passing through towns and villages. Leaving Issoudun, the country road meandered across green pastures populated with placid herds of cows resting under shade trees. It was a peaceful, quiet day, save for the usual creaky noises of wagon wheels grinding down the pebbles littering the dirt road. As usual we moved slowly on our bikes, adjusting our speed to the tempo of the refugees ahead. Suddenly the column in front of us came to a jarring halt, with people jumping off vehicles and running into the fields.

The explanation came swiftly. Closing in fast, a number of low-flying German fighter planes were coming toward us. It was our turn to run for our lives. We only had time to drop our bikes, take a couple of steps and take cover into a providential ditch close to the road before the planes screamed over us. Bursts of deadly machine-gun bullets sprayed the roadway and everything in their path.

Within seconds they were gone. We came out smelling awful but alive, at once realizing we had all laid on ground covered with cow dung. Our reaction was to laugh, as Alice and I were pinching our nostrils in mock disgust. We badly needed some comic relief to calm down from the tense moments we'd gone through.

Although we had escaped, not everyone had fared so well. Several vehicles were burning, with dense smoke casting a dark veil upon us. Not far from us a woman was wounded, lying on the ground, with people around trying to help her. Who knows how many others were wounded or killed by machine-gun fire? The senselessness of the attack made my father decide at once to leave the column of refugees and travel on our own. The alternative was to use country lanes away from the main highways. To be sure, it was a longer and more complicated way to get to St. Savinien, but much safer.

During the following week we rode along narrow dirt lanes with treacherous potholes. While we felt every bump along the way, we never dared to complain, so happy were we to be out of danger. We lost our way many times, without a map to guide us and because of well-intentioned local folks who pointed us in the wrong direction.

Along the way we stopped at small farms for food and shelter. The farmers off the main highway were more hospitable and not as greedy as the ones we'd met before. However, to be fair, they had not encountered hoards of refugees before. At times, some kind farmers invited us to share a hearty meal and a glass of wine. It was impossible to convince them we had traveled from Orleans, such a long distance, on our old and rusty bikes. To them, riding to the next town was already quite a feat.

When we arrived in the town of Montmorillon, my father found a café-tabac establishment. He persuaded the owner, with the help of some extra francs, to sell him a pack of Gauloises without ration coupons. Men sitting at the bar were loudly discussing France's surrender to Germany, blaming defeat upon our spineless government infiltrated by foreign spies, Jews and Bolsheviks. We were stunned by such awful news.

We continued on our way, feeling gloomy and depressed. However, when my father estimated that we would get to St. Savinien in about one week, the prospect of being reunited with my mother and my brother gave me wings.

On the road to St. Savinien, July 1940

We rode into Matha under dark skies and a light drizzle. Arriving at the town center, we found a crowd assembled in the square, silently watching massive German tanks, trucks, motorcycles and other armored vehicles noisily lumbering on the wet and glistening pavement. It was the first time we came face to face with the enemy, the feared *"Boches,"* who had invaded France many times before.

The dark skies echoed our feeling of gloom. I felt dread sweeping over me as I gazed at those hated men in green uniforms. They looked invincible, especially in contrast to the French soldiers riding horsewagons I'd seen in the past. I reluctantly had to admit that the

German soldiers looked so much more lethal with their dark goggles riding their motorized war machines.

After the crowds dispersed, we continued across town. We came upon a slippery, steep cobblestone street and my father skidded, lost his balance and fell hard on the pavement. A man rushed over to help us get him up on his feet. My father was pale and grimaced with pain. He said his right arm hurt. With the aid of the helpful stranger we located a doctor who said my father had fractured his right shoulder and right arm. It was a terrible setback, but my father took the bad news stoically. We had to remain in Matha until my father was outfitted with a plaster cast and was strong enough to get back on the road.

St. Savinien, July 1940

We were excited and filled with joy when the town of St. Savinien came into view. It was as though we'd reached the promised land. Unfortunately, when we arrived at Mrs. Saulnier's house we found out that my mother and brother had not yet arrived.

Mrs. Saulnier was a sprightly elderly woman with a jolly disposition and a hardy laugh. She made us feel at home right away. Nonetheless, it was difficult for us to feel cheery. She had noticed our sad faces and disappointment over my mother's and my brother's absence. She did her best to cheer us up, saying in earnest, "God won't let you down. I'll pray every day to Jesus to watch over your loved ones!"

Mrs. Saulnier lived alone, explaining that she'd been a widow for many years and her grown children were no longer at home. Her modest house was a one-room dwelling, quite similar to many farmhouses we'd seen during our journey across France. Inside there was the usual fieldstone fireplace, a wood stove, a table with benches, an armoire and a bed that completed the Spartan setting. Mrs. Saulnier, expecting the sudden influx of our family, had improvised our sleeping quarters in a shed behind the vegetable garden. "It's not fancy," she conceded. It was quite an understatement, but we were already used to making do without electricity and running water. At least there was a well right outside the shed. We were thankful for anything that made our life a little bit easier.

Since my father's accident, Alice and I had taken turns shaving him. After some shaky beginnings and unsightly nicks that my father chose to ignore, we kept a steadier hand on the long single-blade razor and managed to give him a decent shave.

Our bedding consisted of homemade, lumpy mattresses stuffed with corn husks laid directly on the ground, making crackling noises whenever we moved ever so slightly. The noise was the least of our problems because we were attacked nightly by bugs that had found a home in our mattresses. There was nothing we could do but to endure the bites and scratching. We realized it was the best Mrs. Saulnier could provide for us, and we were not about to complain. On the other hand, she treated us to delicious meals. Mrs. Saulnier took pride in her cooking and served us regional dishes flavored with generous amounts of brandy, not surprising since St. Savinien was in the heart of the Cognac country.

By contrast to the eventful and hectic days spent on the road, the slow and quiet daily pace in St. Savinien was somewhat boring. To keep busy Alice and I were eager to help Mrs. Saulnier run errands and to give her a hand. We pulled weeds in the garden. Alice peeled potatoes, and I hauled wood for the stove and the fireplace. Once in a while my father went to the local café hoping to hear some fresh news. Unfortunately, without radio or newspapers to bring us up to date, we could only speculate about what the future held.

St. Savinien, August 1940

"I have a letter for you," said Mrs. Saulnier as she handed an envelope to my father. I jumped to my feet, my pulse racing wildly. Alice and I were anxiously looking at my father's solemn expression as he carefully slit open the envelope with his pocketknife and extracted a single sheet of paper. The suspense was agonizing, but all of a sudden a broad smile on his face conveyed the good news. "It's from your mother!" my father cried out. Alice and I were laughing and crying at the same time. Mrs. Saulnier had tears in her eyes as she watched us.

We couldn't wait to hear what my mother had written. Were they all right? My father had just finished reading the letter. He turned toward us, his face glowing, "They're both fine," he said. At that moment I felt the dark shadow that had been hovering over us since we left Orleans vanish. Because my mother had written her letter in Yiddish, my father had to translate it for us. She wrote that on the day my father left to get us, she had heard rumors that a bombing of Orleans was imminent. Townspeople were already leaving in droves for the safety of the countryside. She was torn between waiting for our return and joining the exodus. It was really a toss-up. My mother chose to leave the hotel with my brother, and her decision most likely saved their lives. That night a rain of bombs destroyed much of the area of Orleans where she'd been staying.

When Orleans was declared off limits after the bombing, my mother guessed correctly that we would go to St. Savinien. Lacking the strength to take a three-year-old child on such a hazardous journey across France, she felt the only sensible solution was to go back home. Luckily a military ambulance gave her a ride back to Paris. Since that time she had been living in our apartment in Montreuil, worried about our fate but unable to get in touch with us. She hoped we were alive and well in St. Savinien and was anxious to hear from us.

My father wrote back to my mother at once, but because mail was quite slow we didn't expect a reply from her for quite a while. There was actually nothing holding us back in St. Savinien, but we found out that in order to travel by train we had to get travel permits. My father had to go to the town of Saintes, the county seat, to apply for those documents. He was told it would take several weeks for our request to be processed. In the meantime my father went to see the doctor in Matha to have his cast removed. He was happy to find out that his shoulder and right arm were perfectly mended. I had never seen my father so gleeful, swinging his right arm freely.

We left St. Savinien at the end of August, tearfully saying goodbye to the nice Mrs. Saulnier and to our three rusty and faithful bikes, which were put to rest behind the shed.

3

Montreuil, September 1940

Our trip back to Paris was terribly slow, the train stopping numerous times to let German troop transports ahead of us. At almost every station along the way police inspectors came on board to check our travel permits. We finally arrived in Paris at the Montparnasse terminal, weaving our way through a mob of passengers and a sea of green uniforms. Loudpseakers blared announcements in German preceded by *"Achtung!"* (Attention!), one of the many German words I would learn during the occupation. The metro was also crowded with soldiers loudly talking to each other in their guttural-sounding tongue, oblivious of civilians looking at them with sullen expressions.

At last we were back in Montreuil, my heart beating faster as we neared our street. Minutes later I was in my mother's arms, laughing and crying at the same time. We all talked at once, trying to bridge the gap of long months of separation.

Montreuil, October 1940

Since our return from St. Savinien we had not seen even one German soldier in Montreuil. So far the only evidence of the Nazi occupation was the odd sight of long lines of people waiting outside neighborhood stores. Overnight, food had been rationed and quantities were limited. My mother told Alice and me that we would have to pitch in and be prepared to *"faire la queue"* (wait in line), especially at the bakery, butcher and grocery store, to buy our daily staples.

We were issued ration coupons that looked like sheets of stamps, not only for food but also for other scarce items such as wine and tobacco. People began trading with each other. Because we didn't drink wine at home, my mother was able to exchange our coupons to buy cigarettes for my father. Soon after, butter, eggs, cheese, sugar and coffee entirely disappeared and were even difficult to buy on the black market. Instead odd substitutes we called *ersatz* began to appear. Roasted barley replaced coffee, saccharin instead of sugar, and Jerusalem artichokes took the place of potatoes. Every day the list of unpalatable substitutes grew longer.

Montreuil, October 1940

I entered the fifth grade. The boys in my class were no longer as boisterous as in the past. Some of them had fathers or other close relatives who were prisoners in Germany, while others had suffered other tragedies. The war and the occupation already had stamped my generation with a gloomy awareness that pain and sorrow were a part of our lives.

In my classroom a poster-size photograph of Marshal Petain in uniform hung next to my teacher's desk. I had already read that Marshal Petain was one of the most respected military leaders and had fought against Germany during World War I and was considered a national hero.

My new teacher was Mr. Lemonier, a slight balding man who continuously paced around the classroom and made sure that everyone paid close attention to his words.

"We're very lucky that Marshal Petain is our new leader!" he exclaimed, then continued with a long explanation of what had taken place in France since our defeat. Mr. Lemonier said that the Germans were quite magnanimous in allowing our country to have a Frenchman chosen as head of the French government, now located in the town of Vichy.

Mr. Lemonier showed us on a map where the Germans had carved out an area of central France, known as the "non-occupied zone," under the jurisdiction of the Vichy government and Marshal Petain. The rest of France was the "occupied zone," under Nazi control. It included Paris and the northern, eastern and western territories.

From then on every morning in class we all stood at attention facing Marshal Petain's photograph on the wall. Then, with Mr.

Lemonier in the lead, we sung a patriotic hymn honoring him as the savior of France.

Montreuil, November 1940

My parents had to report to the local police precinct to get identification cards for every one of us except my brother, who was under-age. The word "Juif" (Jew) was stamped across the cards in bold red letters. The word Jew made me feel as though I were a criminal. This was a turning point in my life. For the first time I was made explicitly aware of anti-Semitism and of my Jewish identity.

Because my parents were free-thinkers and did not worship or celebrate the Jewish religious holidays, it never occurred to me before that I was any different from other French boys who were Christian.

The topic of religion never came up with my friends. Suddenly I was made to feel like I had a shameful secret to hide from them, and I wondered if they would treat me differently if they discovered that I was Jewish?

Ugly anti-Semitic posters appeared, prominently displayed in Paris's streets and metro. Although I wondered who was responsible for such hateful propaganda against us, my father had no doubt in his mind that the posters were designed by the Nazis to incite the French population against us. One poster I'd seen showed a monster-like creature with a hooked nose carrying a money bag with the star of David, stepping on a woman lying on the ground wearing the French national flag.

Another poster depicted a broom sweeping away rats with hooked noses, with the message in bold type reading, "Sweep away the Jewish vermins!" Even in our quiet neighborhood, where mostly gentiles lived, somebody had scribbled in large letters on a wall: MORT AUX JUIFS! (Death to the Jews). I felt sickened and confused by the posters' portrayal of Jews as money-hungry predators, since my father and his friends were certainly not rich and worked hard to make a living.

Montreuil, March 1941

After a cold and damp winter, spring arrived and lifted our spirits. When anti-Semitic propaganda was not renewed we hoped that the worst was over. But the respite was short lived. We heard through friends that many "rafles" (roundups) of Jewish men were taking place in Paris, carried out by plainclothes French police.

Those sporadic roundups were the beginning of a cycle of fear. The metro became a particular trap for Jews when the French police began making random identification checks in subway cars or blocked the exits, screening all the passengers before they could leave a station.

Montreuil, May 1941

As time went on, the roundups took place everywhere. Public places such as movie houses and theaters became as dangerous as the metro. Those arrested were sent to internment camps run by the French police. We learned there were three such camps, two near Orleans in the towns of Pithiviers and Beaune-la-Rolande, and the third located in the town of Drancy, near Paris.

My parents and their friends viewed with alarm the heightened level of anti-Semitic persecution, and new evidence confirmed that only Jews of foreign origin were targeted by the police. It seemed that at least for the time being the police were staying clear from Jews who were French-born. However, this was not much solace for my parents and their friends, who were facing immediate danger. They heard of an acquaintance who had been arrested and sent to Drancy. His wife was allowed to visit him and to bring him some food. She reported that the conditions there were terrible and degrading. Men were crowded in buildings with no sanitation and no bedding, sleeping on concrete floors, with barely enough food to keep alive, and brutal guards treating them like animals.

My father wisely began to spend most of his time at home repairing watches and fabricating new ones. Sometimes he had no other choice but to travel to Paris to see a customer. On those occasions we were all terribly jittery until he finally came back home. The name "Drancy" struck terror in our hearts, especially when we learned that Jews detained there were being shipped in cattle cars to Germany and to eastern Europe to work in labor camps.

Despite those anxious times Alice and I were able to finish our school year. My parents decided that we would have to forget about our summer vacations in Richebourg. Any travel would be far too risky for my father. Alice and I were disappointed, but we were mature enough to realize that our father's safety came first.

Montreuil, July 1941

Even Bastille Day, usually celebrated with much fanfare on July 14, went by quietly without the usual flag waving, speeches, parades, fireworks and street fairs. There were no French flags on public buildings to mark our independence day, only Nazi flags flying with the swastika, a sober reminder of the defeat of France.

Yet it was difficult to remain pessimistic and gloomy when nature was so gloriously alive on sunny summer days. Alice, Michel and I spent many afternoons with my mother in the green oasis of the park of Vincennes, located within walking distance of our house. We went biking there with my brother following on his tricycle. At times the four of us went rowing around Lake Daumesnil, splashing each other and having a grand time.

Despite the threat of anti-Semitic repression and food shortages, my mother was undaunted. She kept her spirits high by singing and humming arias from her favorite operas. My mother loved company. She was the happiest when people came over and filled our home with noise, conversation and laughter. On many Sunday afternoons my parents' friends would sit around our dining room table, which was laden with fruits, homemade cookies and nuts. Our usual guests were the Pinkowskis, the Friedmans, the Eichenbaums and the Krums. Men sipped schnapps in small shot glasses while the women drank tea. My parents beamed with pride when Alice played piano for their friends, although she had to be coerced to play her entire repertoire of classical pieces.

Staying at home for the summer gave me an opportunity to watch my father at work. He always wore an immaculate starched white smock and, with his serious demeanor, he reminded me of a doctor. He was extremely meticulous, his tools perfectly lined up on his rolltop desk like little soldiers. All the watch parts were neatly stored in clear cellophane envelopes and placed in little drawers.

My father was usually bent over his desktop looking through a magnifying glass to pick up tiny watch parts and fit them together like a miniature puzzle. I tried not to disturb him, but my curiosity was such that I often peppered him with many questions, which he patiently answered. My father seemed pleased by my eagerness to learn about his work. Such close work required total concentration from him. Once in a while he took a break, lit a Gauloise and leaned back in his chair. With eyes half-shut he slowly exhaled puffs of smoke that spiraled upward in a bluish haze.

Montreuil, October 1941

Alice and I returned to school and were able to resume our studies despite the lingering threat of anti-Semitism. It seemed at times the occupation was over, especially in our quiet neighborhood, where German soldiers hardly ventured.

Unfortunately they were everywhere else. We only had to read newspapers to be reminded that the Nazis almost ruled Europe, having defeated one nation after another. The Soviet Union was in near collapse, as evidenced by photographs of captured Russian soldiers, destroyed military material and bombed cities. It was as though no power on earth could stop Germany. Despite those grim reports, my father was optimistic that one day the tide would turn against them. "It's all Nazi propaganda! Besides with all their boasting they have yet to defeat England."

General de Gaulle had fled to London rather than collaborate with the enemy. Through short-wave radio broadcasts he exhorted French patriots to fight back, thus becoming a symbol of resistance against the Nazis. We cheered when we heard of the partisans' daring raids and sabotage against German troops. Unfortunately the Nazis swiftly retaliated, killing hundreds of French hostages for the death of one of their men.

The hostages' names were listed by the German "Kommandantur," posted in Paris' streets and metro. Those notices, printed on a yellow background with black type, were chilling reminders of their death, making people feel angry and helpless. Besides fearing the

Nazis my parents and their friends were shocked to hear that six synagogues in Paris had been bombed and set ablaze by French right-wing fascists. It seemed that every time we believed that anti-Semitism was abating, new incidents rekindled our fears.

Montreuil, December 1941

The entry into the war by the United States was reported by the Nazi-controlled press as though it were a trivial occurrence. My father, who prided himself as a student of history, was overjoyed by this news. He remembered World War I, when in 1918 the United States joined France and England and helped defeat Germany. He was hopeful that history would repeat itself.

The German occupation and food shortages contributed to make the Christmas holiday quite depressing. Even though my parents did not celebrate this holiday, I missed the festivities of years past, when Paris was resplendent with lights and the largest department stores presented special Christmas displays for children. It was a time when my mother took Alice and me to Paris to see those fabulous creations. As we emerged from the metro we found long lines that stretched for blocks. We waited in line with other children bundled up against the cold. Patiently moving along the sidewalk, we craned our necks to catch a glimpse of fairytale settings with lifelike puppets moving about. Alice and I were completely awed and transfixed by such magic.

Christmas day came along. I was thrilled to get a birthday present from my parents, two adventure books that were on my wish list: *The Last of the Mohicans* and *Twenty Thousand Leagues Under the Sea*.

Montreuil, February 1942

Long lines at our neighborhood stores tested everybody's patience and nerves. With less foodstuff available, ration coupons became as precious as money, and counterfeit coupons available on the black market cost a small fortune. To make up for the shortages my school distributed daily vitamin supplements in the form of odd-tasting candies and biscuits. At home my mother improvised meals with whatever food was available that day. She resorted to making vegetable stews with rutabagas, a potato substitute we all loathed but had to tolerate. Eventually, even with coupons we could not find butter, cheese, eggs and poultry.

My parents had kept in touch with the kind Mrs. Balossier in Richebourg, where we had spent many happy vacations. She was on good terms with local farmers and able to get for us those dairy products and poultry that had disappeared from store shelves. Getting to Richebourg presented a problem because my father could not take such a risk, and my mother had to stay home with my brother. I was proud that my parents entrusted me with this mission and allowed me to travel on my own. Despite first-time jitters, I did as well as could be expected. Even Mrs. Balossier was impressed by the way I handled the entire transaction, "Like a grown-up," she said. I returned home with a heavy knapsack replete with fresh farm provisions. I did so well on my first trip that my parents sent me several more times to Richebourg to replenish our food supply.

Like any other adult I had to carry my ID card, except that mine identified me as a Jew. I didn't worry that the police would bother me because of my young age. However, once my cockiness was put to a test. The train was crowded, with barely enough room to put down my heavy knapsack. At one of the many stops on my way back to Paris, two policemen came on board, randomly checking passengers' ID cards. They slowly wove their way in my direction until one policeman stopped right in front of me.

"ID card please!" he said, thrusting his hand in my direction, his eyes staring at me. I froze, my heart pounding in my chest, barely able to move. I suddenly remembered that my ID card was in my knapsack. Trembling, I was about to get it when I felt someone's hand brushing over my head as the policeman grabbed the ID card from the man standing behind me.

Montreuil, May 1942

Jews were notified that they were forbidden to be out between the hours of 8:00 P.M. and 6:00 A.M. We were not only humiliated, we also shuddered to think that such sanctions might follow. Soon after, another police ordinance struck us with gloom. We were told to wear a "Jewish star," to be sewn on all our outer clothing, the failure to obey was punishable by imprisonment. The six-pointed stars were yellow with black borders and the word "Juif" boldly printed in black, the letters shaped to resemble Hebrew characters. They were issued at our police precinct. My mother spent hours sewing all those patches on our clothing.

Alice and I felt terribly self-conscious having to wear the Jewish star in public. Our parents tried to comfort us, saying that we had nothing to be ashamed of. It was still difficult to keep our composure outside under people's sharp stares. On my way to school I hid the star by holding my schoolbag close to my chest, but once there I could no longer escape the scrutiny of the other boys.

Few Jews lived in my neighborhood, and I did not fit my schoolmates' image of a Jew, which was fueled by anti-Semitic propaganda of a monster with horns and tail. Many boys from my class reassured me they were still my friends, while others pushed and kicked me in the hallway, taunting me and calling me *"youpin"* (kike) behind my back.

My sixth grade teacher, Mr. Manceaux, sternly reprimanded those mean-spirited kids, reminding them to practice Christian charity.

Montreuil, June 1942

Other anti-Semitic police ordinances followed. We learned that we were barred from many public places, such as movies and theaters. Every day the list grew longer. Notices appeared warning the public of the restrictions. It seemed as though our world was closing in around us as we watched our civil rights disappear. Despite those trying times Alice and I managed to finish school. I graduated with honors from the sixth grade, making my parents proud with my *certificat d'études primaires* diploma.

Montreuil, July 1942

Bastille Day, July 14, marked the end of school and the start of summer vacation. It was too risky to go away, and though Alice and I were somewhat disappointed, we had yet to know that lack of vacations would be the least of our concerns.

On July 16 my mother had an appointment in Paris with her

dentist, who was also Jewish. He told my mother that one of his long-time patients who was a policeman had warned him that he and hundreds of fellow officers were on alert for the night of July 16 to roundup every Jew from Paris and its suburbs. Convinced that this was true, my mother immediately invited her good friends the Krums to come and stay with us until the threat of a roundup was over. She felt that it would be easier to find a hiding place in our neighborhood, where fewer Jews lived than in Paris.

Alice and I were happy and surprised to see my mother with Mr. and Mrs. Krum and Joseph. We had no idea that they would be staying with us. However, we soon learned it was not at all a social call and were dumfounded to hear what my mother had to tell us. My father, skeptical, was not yet convinced that the threat was real.

The Krums finally tipped the argument in my mother's favor, telling my father that we couldn't afford to take a chance. The next challenge was finding a hiding place. My mother persuaded her cleaning woman, Mrs. Canestrier, who lived nearby, to let us stay in her house until the danger had passed. Before leaving we took the precaution of removing our Jewish stars from our clothing. On our way my mother alerted the two other Jewish families in our building of the impending roundup. We spent the night packed in a small room, fitfully waiting for morning to come.

As daylight slowly filtered into the room, I wondered what we would learn. My parents prudently waited until the afternoon to send me to our house and report back if it was safe to return. The streets were quiet, without any sign of police presence. Another false alarm I thought, remembering my father's earlier skepticism. I pressed the buzzer. Our concierge pulled me inside her apartment, quickly shutting the door behind us. She was edgy, looking toward her window as though she expected someone. Mrs. Ackerman finally uttered with a deep sigh, *"Mon pauvre petit garçon!"* (My poor little boy!). My heart sank, already guessing the bad news she had to tell.

She wearily sat down and proceeded to tell me that the police had come during the early morning hours. "I never expected Frenchmen to be as cruel as Nazis," she said, her eyes filling with tears. She related how the tragic events had unfolded. A team of policemen woke her up, demanding to see each apartment occupied by Jewish tenants. An officer showed her a list of names, including ours. Mrs. Ackerman had to show the way and open each apartment with her passkey. She was relieved to find ours empty.

Unfortunately some of our Jewish neighbors did not fare as well by remaining home. They were given only minutes to dress and pack up some clothing, then were escorted to a city bus, which was parked outside and filled with other arrested Jewish families. Mrs. Ackerman said she was still haunted by the cries of young children. I shuddered, thinking the Krums and my family could have been on that bus. Fate had decided otherwise.

"Don't worry, we'll grab those Jews sooner or later!" said a policeman after finding our apartment empty. She told me to warn my parents that the police could be back at any time. Despite the danger, my parents and the Krums went back to retrieve some valuables and clothing. We couldn't stay much longer with Mrs. Canestrier, fearing that a snoopy neighbor might denounce her to the police or the Gestapo for hiding Jews.

Our situation looked terribly grim until we were rescued by two merchants, neighbors from Vincennes with whom my mother had kept close ties. Aware of our plight, they kept us hidden in their stores' back rooms, where no one was aware of our presence. We first stayed in the Lefèvre's hardware store and then in Mrs. Garnier's pharmacy. For a short while we were safe, but I wondered how long those compassionate gentiles could keep us hidden.

We slept on blankets laid on hard cement floors and ate whatever our hosts could spare for us. During store hours we were careful to keep our voices low so people would not hear us. Time moved ever so slowly in the close confines of those cluttered storage rooms. There were no windows, only bulbs casting a dim light upon our weary faces. Days eventually blended into nights. Alice, Joseph and I devised quiet games to ward off our boredom and keep our minds off our fear that we might be discovered. Only thin walls separated us from customers on the other side. My mother did her best to soothe my restless brother and keep him from crying. My parents and the Krums somehow managed to keep an optimistic outlook, despite the fact that soon we had to move out without any other prospects. Providence must have heard our pleas because suddenly a stranger named Mrs. Bonneau entered our lives.

She lived in the neighborhood and was a long-time customer at the pharmacy. Mrs. Garnier knew that she could be trusted. Mrs. Bonneau was told about our terrible predicament and of the urgent need to find another hiding place for us. She promised to help and a couple of days later returned, informing Mrs. Garnier that she and her husband had worked out a plan to save us.

The Bonneaus' house was only a couple of blocks away from the pharmacy. A two-story stone structure with a small garden next to it, set back behind a metal fence. Mrs. Bonneau expected us. She was a slender middle-aged woman who appeared at the front door with two white poodles jumping at her sides.

She led us to the front parlor, where we met her husband, her daughter and a dapper, thirtyish man by the name of Mr. Ernst, who was introduced as a trusted family friend. Mr. Bonneau, a tall balding man in his fifties, had an aristocratic bearing, sporting a gray mustache and a manicured beard. His daughter, Madeleine, was a cheerful young-looking woman in her twenties with blond hair and clear blue eyes.

After brief introductions my parents and Mr. and Mrs. Krum huddled in one side of the room, anxiously listening to Mr. and Mrs. Bonneau tell them what they had planned for us. Mr. Bonneau's deep voice rose in earnest as he declared, "Don't worry, my good people, rest assured we'll look after your children as though they were our own."

Mr. and Mrs. Bonneau believed we all stood a better chance of escaping by going our separate ways. Since time was of the essence they already had arranged to have Joseph, Michel and me placed with their friend Mr. Ernst in his home town of St. Aubin-les-Elbeuf, near Rouen, with his mother ready to look after my younger brother.

As for Alice, the Bonneaus had yet to find a safe place for her. A few days later quite unexpectedly a solution came along, thanks to Mrs. Bronzini, a laundress from our neighborhood. My mother had used her services for many years and considered her more a friend than an employee. When she found out that Mrs. Bronzini and her family were leaving for their summer vacation to the country, she asked her to take my sister with them as a favor.

The Bonneau's intervention was miraculous, but it felt strange. Since the roundup my parents and the Krums had made all the crucial decisions that kept us free, and suddenly we had to trust the judgment of strangers for our survival. I didn't know for sure what my parents and the Krums were planning to do, although they had discussed the possibility of escaping to the "non-occupied" zone, which was considered a safe place for Jews.

With such a flurry of activity, I had little time left to ponder or fear what the future held in store for us. Deep down I was convinced that my family, who had already overcome so many hurdles, would somehow prevail. Within days we all took different paths. Michel was the first one to leave with Mr. Ernst. Then Alice joined Mrs. Bronzini. Mr. Ernst finally returned, taking Joseph and me to his hometown in Normandy.

As Joseph and I left the Bonneau's house, I looked back one more time at the parlor window where my parents and the Krums were posted, waving to us a last goodbye. I waved back, drying my tears, hurrying along to catch up with the waiting Mr. Ernst.

In Hiding

4

St. Aubin-les-Elbeuf, August 1942

Mr. Ernst, Joseph and I took the metro to the Gare St. Lazare station. It was the first time I had stepped outside since the roundup, nervously facing a new and hostile world. Everything around me still had the same familiar look, but the couple of weeks spent in hiding had made me wary and more alert to potential dangers. On the metro I was particularly aware of occasional glances in my direction from other passengers. Could anyone guess that Joseph and I were fugitives running away from the police, I wondered? I tried to reason that anyone looking at us had to assume we were going camping, since we were wearing shorts and carrying knapsacks.

Nonetheless I heaved a sigh of relief when we had made it safely to the station and found seats on a crowded train headed for St. Aubin-les-Elbeuf, a town on the Seine River about eighty miles northwest of Paris. At one of the stops several policemen came into our car. I instantly felt my pulse racing, as I thought about the recent close call I had had coming back from Richebourg.

Joseph paled, also aware of the police standing nearby, only a few feet away from us. There was nothing we could do but pretend that we were two carefree boys on their way to summer camp. Meanwhile Mr. Ernst looked relaxed, entertaining us with small talk, not paying any attention to the policemen around us. Mr. Ernst was a handsome man with fine features and glossy black hair carefully combed back. He was obviously aware of his good looks and of the attention he was getting, smiling back at women sitting across the aisle.

After crossing the congested Paris suburbs we traveled through the lush and picturesque Normandy countryside dotted with small villages and farmlands stretching to the horizon. Despite my earlier qualms, we reached St. Aubin-les-Elbeuf without an incident or another cause for alarm. Mr. Ernst's younger brothers were waiting for us outside the station, two gangly young men puffing on cigarette butts. They wore rumpled overalls and dust-coated rubber boots, in sharp contrast to their older brother's elegant tweed suit and shiny leather shoes.

We followed them to a battered pickup truck parked nearby. Mr. Ernst sat in front with his brothers, while Joseph and I found some room in the back between piles of junk. After a short ride through town we continued along a rise overlooking the Seine River below. Soon there were fewer houses and more stretches of farmland. We stopped in front of a two-story house isolated from its neighbors, set back behind a rusty iron fence with rambling vegetation.

Before I was able to step out of the truck, Michel came racing out of the front door and threw himself into my arms, tears freely running down his cheeks. He held on to me tightly, laughing and crying at the same time. "You are staying with me. Promise!" he said. I nodded, squeezing his body against mine. I felt sad for my brother because even as a bright five-year-old child he couldn't possibly appreciate why we had been separated from our parents.

We stepped inside the house. The smells of cooking and musty old furniture blended together. Joseph and I were greeted by Mr. Ernst's mother, a thin, middle-aged woman with graying hair who came shuffling along, followed by a small dog ferociously barking behind the safety of her dress. Mrs. Ernst looked us over, appraising us with small inquisitive eyes. I was not able to tell by her laconic expression whether we made a good impression upon her. She took us upstairs to our bedroom, a cubicle with two beds and a dresser. She pointed to a washbowl on the dresser and a chamber pot on the floor, for our toilet and nightly needs. Modern plumbing, running water and indoor bathrooms, had yet to come to this rural area.

Mrs. Ernst said I would share the same bed with my brother and rather abruptly told me to look after him, to make sure he didn't wet the bedsheets again. I was really surprised to hear her complaint, because I couldn't recall Michel wetting the bed since he was much younger. He turned red as a beet, with nowhere to hide when Mrs. Ernst held the chamber pot to his face and began to lecture him. I said I was sorry it had happened, trying to appease her and defuse the situation.

Despite her stern warning, my brother had another "accident" during the night. I told him to stop crying or he would wake up the entire household. I promptly stripped the bed and hung the sheets outside the window to dry. Fortunately for us the summer nights were balmy. By morning the bedsheets were dry and the smell hardly detectable.

About a week later Mr. Ernst informed me that my brother would be placed with another family in St. Aubin-les-Elbeuf, because his mother had complained that she was not up to the task of looking after a young child. Seeing my consternation, Mr. Ernst tried to reassure me: "Those people are close friends of mine, fully aware that your brother is Jewish and willing to give him a loving and safe home. Don't worry, you'll be able to see him from time to time." Feeling dejected, I wondered how Michel would take the news.

The day arrived when Mr. Ernst's friend, a man named Mr. Leclère, came over to pick up my brother. Michel was disconsolate, crying and clinging to me. I managed to calm him down by painting a rosy picture of his future home, telling him how lucky he was to be rid of the "witch" he feared so much (an apt nickname he had chosen for Mrs. Ernst). Michel tried to put on a brave face for my benefit, but couldn't quite succeed. Tears still bathed his cheeks.

We waited outside for Mr. Leclère, a tall, slender man in his early forties wearing a corduroy jacket and a floppy cap. He dismounted from his bike, which was attached to a box-like trailer, and shook hands with Mr. Ernst and me and gently patted Michel on the head. His kind expression gave me some hope that my brother would be in good hands with him. I hugged Michel as he sat in the bike trailer holding his small suitcase on his lap. Then Mr. Leclère pedaled away. Michel waved to me with a big smile on his face, suddenly excited at the prospect of a fun ride.

After our separation I was lucky to have some opportunities to visit my brother. The Leclères lived close by in a small white stucco house set behind a short brick wall and a manicured flower garden. The interior of the house was equally neat and welcoming. The household consisted of Mr. and Mrs. Leclère and Gaston, their six-teen-year-old son. It cheered me to find Michel looking happier than before, laughing and already feeling at home with them. I was touched to see Mrs. Leclère fuss over him and to see Gaston, like a big brother, carry Michel on his back. Mr. Leclère worked in a near-by textile plant, and Gaston was an apprentice butcher. They were hard-working people, and despite modest means they generously bought my brother some new clothes and a pair of shoes.

After I kissed my mother goodbye she had stuck into my pock-et a handful of "sous" (pennies), "to buy treats," she said. I was glad that I hadn't squandered my money on candies but had instead bought some inexpensive little toys for my brother, which I brought to him one at a time during each visit, so that they would last. Michel proudly kept them neatly displayed in the living room on a dresser.

I felt the Leclères couldn't have been nicer to my brother; yet at times he was restless and moody, longing for our parents and Alice, asking the same question over and over: "How soon are we going home?" I couldn't possibly tell Michel I didn't know; as his big brother, I was supposed to have all the answers. I made up optimis-tic guesses to keep him happy, all along wishing it would be so.

After several weeks living under the same roof as the Ernst fam-ily, Joseph and I still had no clue about Mr. Ernst's and his brothers' lines of work. Although it was none of our business, we were in-trigued because they kept quiet about their work. We were too well brought up to ask them questions. Albert and Jerome often took off early in their pickup truck, returning home at dusk just before the curfew imposed by the Germans. Mr. Ernst too, was gone for days at a time.

Joseph thought something was *louche* (fishy) about them. "What if Albert and Jerome were crooks?" I argued back. "Just be-cause they act strangely and keep to themselves doesn't make it so." Joseph was unimpressed with my views, saying, "I still think they're hiding something from us." Being older than I was, a little more than three years my senior, Joseph thought I should defer to his judgement. Although I resented this aloof manner and condescend-ing treatment, I reluctantly had to admit that he was quite smart.

We didn't have long to wait to test Joseph's theory, for one evening Albert and Jerome asked for our help in unloading their truck. They lifted the heavy tarpaulin, and stacks of bicycles appeared before us. I was startled. Joseph gave me a knowing and conspiratorial wink. We took the bikes one by one down to the darkened basement. Albert led with a flashlight and unlocked a door opening into a large room filled with more bikes lined up in neat rows. It was like stepping into a bike store with wheels, tires and other spare parts hanging from hooks. Questions rushed through my mind. Was it possible that Joseph had guessed right? Were Albert and Jerome thieves operating on their own? Or were they part of a ring, or just fences hiding stolen merchandise?

Joseph couldn't wait to be alone with me to show off. "Didn't I tell you they were thieves?" he said, beaming. Of course, Albert and Jerome probably knew we were hiding in their house from the police and had nothing to fear from us telling someone about their business. Joseph continued, "Do you have any idea how much a bike costs today, even a used one on the black market?" I had no idea, but I knew that it had to be a lot. "But there's one piece of the puzzle still missing—Mr. Ernst!" Joseph said, comically fluttering one eyebrow, an involuntary tic he had when concentrating.

Joseph didn't have to bother honing his detective skills, because a couple of days later the missing piece of the puzzle fell into place by itself. On that day Joseph and I were posted outside by Mr. Ernst to act as lookouts for "an important delivery" he said he was expecting, and he told us to report to him promptly if any strangers were seen loitering near the house. Thus we finally learned the nature of his business. Mr. Ernst bought cattle and sold beef on the black market. He had many accomplices, farmers who trucked in live steers to a large shed in his back yard, (the "strangers" we were on the lookout for), and butchers who slaughtered the animals and quartered the meat to be sold. To be sure, Mr. Ernst was not a thief like his brothers, but he was an enterprising—if not a shady—businessman.

St. Aubin-les-Elbeuf, September 1942

After discovering Mr. Ernst's business, Joseph was clearly worried. "Dealing in the black market is illegal, but slaughtering cattle reserved for German troops is a crime," he said. He concluded that if the police or Germans got wind of Mr. Ernst's little business operation, not only would Mr. Ernst and his family be arrested, but so would we, and our Jewish identity would be revealed. I was depressed and angry at Joseph for painting such a bleak picture in my mind, but I was chilled by its accuracy.

Outside of those occasions when we were summoned to help Mr. Ernst and his brothers, we were free to do as we pleased as long as we stayed inside the house. We spent the time reading, talking, and playing cards. Joseph wrote a journal. Some passages were hilarious, especially those concerning the Ernsts. He didn't spare anyone from his usual sarcastic humor. He described Mrs. Ernst as *"la vieille fouine"* (the old weasel). Albert and Jerome earned the nicknames *"voyou numéro un et voyou numéro deux"* (riffraff number one and riffraff number two). Mr. Ernst fared better as *"Monsieur quatre épingles"* (Mister spic-and-span).

Even though Joseph made fun of our hosts, we had no reason to complain of the way we were treated. We even managed to overlook Mrs. Ernst's surliness because of the excellent meals she prepared. Meat was never in short supply. We all ate in the kitchen, Mrs. Ernst serving each person quickly and efficiently. There was hardly any talk at dinnertime, only the clatter of utensils and the sounds of chewing and slurping. Mr. Ernst occasionally broke the silence with some compliments for his mother's fine cooking. It was a mystery to me why Mr. Ernst was so different from his brothers; he was refined and outgoing, in contrast to their awkward and provincial ways.

At times I thought Joseph worried too much. He tried to convince me we faced imminent danger unless we took some action. His doomsday prophecy was "We'll have no one else to blame if the police or the Germans come to arrest us." That kind of gloomy talk made me nervous. Besides, I couldn't imagine what other choice we had but to remain with the Ernst family. Joseph proposed that we send a letter to the Bonneaus asking to be relocated. I reluctantly agreed, wondering how we could make our case without implicating the Ernsts.

Joseph expected me to rally to his side, but I had to remind him that before we left Vincennes, Mr. Bonneau had told us not to write.

"We have to be extra careful," he said. In the event that we had to get in touch, Mr. Ernst would contact the Bonneaus.

Joseph was not swayed and dismissed my protest as a feeble argument. "Don't you see we're in trouble?" he asked. I knew in my heart that he was right, but I was fearful that we would make the Bonneaus angry. "I can't possibly leave my brother," I countered, trying one more time to make him change his mind. It was to no avail; he was relentless until I agreed that writing to the Bonneaus was the right course of action. Joseph promptly composed an emotional letter about how unhappy we were with the Ernst family, but he never alluded to their shady activities. At the last minute he changed his mind about writing the letter himself, saying the Bonneaus would be more receptive toward our request if it came from me because I was the youngest. I thought this was another of Joseph's tricks and that he wanted me to take the blame in case our plan backfired. But Joseph made me see his way once more, and I reluctantly wrote the letter.

A couple of weeks after I wrote the letter, Madeleine Bonneau unexpectedly arrived in St. Aubin-les-Elbeuf. She was friendly and cheerful, just the way I'd remembered her. She did not hint at why she had come. She talked for a while with Mr. Ernst, then announced she was taking me back to Vincennes, having made some arrangements for me. Finding a place for Joseph had to wait a while longer. I felt sorry for Joseph, who had started the entire process and who was now left behind. I quickly ran over to the Leclères to say goodbye to Michel, my heart filled with sadness as I realized that I might not see him for a long time. My only consolation was knowing he was in good hands.

During our trip back to Vincennes, Madeleine Bonneau told me her parents had been touched by my letter, and they believed I must have been terribly unhappy if I had contacted them directly. I was relieved to know that Mr. and Mrs. Bonneau were not angry with me. With an impish look on her face, Madeleine said she had a surprise for me: "You should be happy to learn that my parents made arrangements for you and your sister to be sent together to a safe place in Normandy."

I was elated upon hearing such wonderful news. The only cloud marring this joyful moment was that I did not have any news about my parents. Madeleine said they were still waiting to hear from them. I suddenly felt dejected, and was unable to hide my disappointment. With a warm smile, Madeleine told me to cheer up, and gently pressed my hands in hers. She said she understood my anxiety, but urged me to take heart. She reminded me that it had not been such a long time since my parents and the Krums left Vincennes, and told me sending mail from the "non-occupied" zone was probably difficult. Madeleine's optimism and cheerfulness were hard to resist, and soon I was feeling more hopeful about the future.

From the metro to Madeleine's house was a short walk along streets familiar from my earlier childhood. For a brief moment I relived the tense days following the July roundup, when I had questioned my safety. Arriving at the Bonneaus' home, I suddenly felt I was back in a safe harbor. It was wonderful to be warmly greeted by Mr. and Mrs. Bonneau, but best of all was being reunited with my sister.

5

Vincennes, September 1942

Alice and I remained with the Bonneaus until we were relocated to Normandy. Even though it was a brief stay, we were able to gather some insight into the Bonneaus' background. We'd assumed all along that they were Catholic, like most French people. We were mistaken. The Bonneaus told us they belonged to a Protestant church called the Huguenots. They were proud of their affiliation and explained that, unlike Catholics, who shunned other religions, their religion was liberal and progressive. "We are Christians but respect other religious beliefs, like your own," said Mr. Bonneau.

From the time that we were young children Alice was an avid reader, able to recall the most arcane subjects with facts and figures at her fingertips. And so it didn't come as a surprise to me that she already knew a great deal about the Huguenots. She remembered reading that this small Protestant sect had begun flourishing in France as an offshoot of Calvinism during the sixteenth-century. Even though the Huguenots were a religious minority, they were seen as a threat by the Catholic church because of their enlightened views and democratic ways. As a result, Huguenots in the past had been persecuted and massacred by the Catholic church.

Huguenots in France no longer feared for their lives and were free to practice their religion. Yet Alice wondered if the Bonneaus felt a special kinship with us because of the past history of Huguenot persecution. Regardless of their motives, we owed them much!

The Bonneaus must have had some money, for they owned a car, a luxury few could afford. Mr. Bonneau proudly showed us his black Citroen, now sitting lifeless in the side yard. He cursed the Germans for making it impossible to use his beloved car. We learned that Mr. Bonneau was a mechanical engineer and the manager of a small manufacturing concern. He was quite cosmopolitan, having traveled to England frequently before the war on business and pleasure. He had adopted the British custom of drinking tea and eating bacon and eggs for breakfast—before rationing took place, of course. Mr. Bonneau also had great admiration for the British people for resisting the Nazis, unlike France, which had given up without a fight. As for Mrs. Bonneau, she remained in the background, letting her husband enjoy the spotlight. She seemed happy to defer to him, except in the kitchen or the dining room, where she was clearly in charge. Despite rationing we enjoyed the abundant meals she elegantly served on her best china.

The day came when the Bonneaus told us that they had arranged for a trusted friend to take us to Normandy, where we would be safe from the prying eyes of the police and the Gestapo. They said despite their best efforts, they couldn't place us together. However, they found two families in the same village who were willing to take us. As for Michel, they thought that it was best to leave him with the Leclères, who were taking such good care of him. Mr. Bonneau wanted to make sure we understood that the farmers who would take us in had not been told that we were Jewish, merely that we were needy city children. He didn't tell us whether those farmers would be paid to keep us. Nor did he say that we would be expected to help with the farm chores.

There was not much else to be said, except for a parting comment from Mrs. Bonneau, who reminded us not to write to Michel or to them: "Don't worry, my dear children, we'll do our best from time to time to get in touch with you." Madeleine had taken time off from work to see us off, and she said she was going to miss us. Alice and I were ready to go. We carried knapsacks with the few items of clothing that had been retrieved after the roundup.

The Bonneaus' friend arrived. I had expected to see an older person like them, not the pert and fashionably dressed young woman who came in. She embraced us warmly. I instantly fell under her charm. Her name was Mrs. Mounier. She was in her late twenties, slender, with wavy blond hair framing her pretty face.

We took the metro to the Montparnasse station, a familiar place that Alice and I had traveled through many times on our way to

Richebourg. Mrs. Mounier informed us that we were going to Savigny-le-Vieux, a village in western Normandy. I remembered from my geography lessons that this region was near the province of Brittany. During the long train ride, Mrs. Mounier kept us entertained with stories and jokes, almost making us forget our anxieties about what lay ahead.

There was no direct connection to Savigny-le-Vieux. We got off the train in the city of Laval and boarded a rickety bus to the town of Fougerolles-du-Plessis. It was dark by the time we arrived. We waited at the bus stop until a short woman carrying a lantern walked up to us and inquired if we were the folks from Paris. We were happy that we'd found her.

She said her name was Mrs. Ledauphin, but asked us to call her Madeleine, like everyone else did. The light from her lantern revealed a pleasant-looking woman in her mid-thirties, with dark hair, wearing a large apron over a black dress. We followed her to a cart harnessed to a large horse tied to a post. Mrs. Ledauphin greeted her horse with a gentle pat on the rump and a jovial *"Bonjour ma Jolie!"* (Hello my pretty!). The mare neighed back a sonorous welcome.

We climbed in the cart and pressed together on a narrow bench. Mrs. Ledauphin tugged the reins, and la Jolie lurched forward, first slowly across town, then faster on a darkened country road. Mrs. Ledauphin cheerfully chatted with us in her peculiar patois, which was often hard to follow over the creaking noise of wheels grinding on the rough pavement.

She told us that she had two children: a girl, Solange, who was fourteen like my sister; and a young boy Wilfrid, who was five. Her husband, Marcel, served in the French army and had been captured with his unit. He was now held in a prison camp in Germany. "It's more than two years that Marcel has been gone!" she sighed. She conceded that running the farm without her husband was difficult, but somehow she had managed to keep it going, thanks to her neighbors, who lent her a hand at harvest time.

She turned toward Mrs. Mounier, saying she was glad she had brought Alice, because she was looking for a companion for her daughter and for someone to help her with chores around the farm.

I then realized that Alice was to stay with Mrs. Ledauphin. I was happy for my sister because this woman seemed genuinely nice, but I also felt envious of her good fortune.

We reached the village of Savigny-le-Vieux. Dark houses were swallowed by the inky night, with only the faint glow of candlelight filtering through shutters. But we had not yet reached our destination. Mrs. Ledauphin told us her farm was a bit farther, a couple of miles up the road, in the hamlet of Alleray.

We finally arrived. The courtyard was filled with smells of burning wood and cow manure. We walked into the farmhouse, where Mrs. Ledauphin's children and her helper had stayed up long after their bedtime to greet us. We sat for a while around the fireplace in the glow of red embers, relaxing from our long trip and getting acquainted. I kept my fingers crossed, hoping my future home would be as friendly as this one.

Savigny-le-Vieux

6

La Châtaigneraie, September 1942
The next morning, Mrs. Ledauphin hitched La Jolie to the cart to take me to my new home, a farm in the nearby hamlet of La Châtaigneraie. Mrs. Mounier came along to meet my future family, while Alice stayed behind to help Solange with some chores. I waved goodbye to my sister, wondering how soon I would be able to see her again.

We went on our way, Mrs. Ledauphin guiding La Jolie along a cow path and skillfully avoiding getting stuck in the deep ruts carved in the ground. We meandered through pastures and apple orchards partially hidden behind hedgerows capped with trees and thick vegetation. There was little sign of life other than herds of cows and sheep grazing. Every so often we rode by religious icons, ancient stone crucifixes erected on crooked pedestals. At each icon Mrs. Ledauphin quickly crossed herself.

It seemed that we rode for a long time, even though the distance was not more than three miles from the Ledauphin's farm to the hamlet of La Châtaigneraie. Mrs. Ledauphin told us she seldom came that way and knew little about Mrs. Huard, the woman with whom I was to stay, except that her husband was also a prisoner of war. "So many women today have to struggle alone. I am sure she'll be glad to have some extra help," Mrs. Ledauphin said to me. It was the first time I realized I would be expected to do work like a hired hand.

We came upon a jumble of farmhouses and barns. We pulled into a courtyard, our arrival greeted by a chorus of cackling hens and two mean-looking dogs barking and baring their teeth. Mrs. Huard, a tall wiry woman in her thirties, came to greet us with a thin little girl in tow whom she introduced as her daughter Josette. A farmhand who was loading up hay soon joined us, anxious to have a closer look at the visitors. His name was Antoine, a sturdy-looking young man I guessed to be in his late teens, with wild whiskers sprouting on his jutting chin.

We followed Mrs. Huard into the farmhouse. She offered us some cider. Mrs. Mounier took her aside, and they spoke for a while. I assumed they were speaking about me, because from time to time Mrs. Huard glanced in my direction, her small round eyes appraising me. I wondered if she was disappointed that I was not the robust youth she might have expected, but instead a slender city boy who was an unlikely candidate for hard work. I turned to Josette. She looked a lot like her mother, with frizzy brown hair and small round eyes. She was ten, and although I tried to make conversation, she shyly retreated into her shell.

Mrs. Mounier told me everything was settled with Mrs. Huard. She whispered, "I am sure you'll do your best to help her. I'll be back soon, hopefully in a couple of months, to see how you and your sister are faring." I didn't know who this wonderful Mrs. Mounier was, but to me she was like an angel watching over us. She gave me a last hug, and I rejoined Mrs. Huard.

For the next couple of weeks I followed Antoine around to familiarize myself with the many tasks he did, since he said some of them I soon would have to carry out on my own. He showed me the land owned by Mrs. Huard. It was a relatively small parcel of apple orchards, stretches of pastures, and wheat, rye, corn and potato fields planted to provide feed for the animals. There were two horses, about a dozen cows and calves, sheep, pigs and barnyard residents to look after. While I quickly found my way around, it took me a while longer to get used to the lingering acrid smells of cow and horse manure.

I struggled at first to understand Antoine's thick rural patois. He was a simple country boy with little education, who never traveled beyond the next town, where he had been born, hired to do the heavy work that Mrs. Huard's husband would have done. I found him to be easygoing and friendly with me, and uncomplaining and patient with the animals. His ruddy complexion and strong, calloused hands attested to his years of outdoor life on the farm.

The farmhouse was similar to the houses of Mrs. Huard's neighbors. It was a small, one-story building, with whitewashed walls and a steep roof covered with thick layers of straw. Next to it were the stables and a barn where I shared a bed with Antoine. Across the yard other smaller structures housed sheep, pigs, chicken coops and rabbit cages, and beyond those were brick ovens, a shed holding a cider press, a well, stacks of logs and tall piles of kindling wood.

The interior of the farmhouse was typical, with a hard-packed dirt floor and a low-beamed ceiling, a stone fireplace with the usual array of cooking utensils and a cauldron, pots and skillets blackened with soot. It was sparsely furnished with a massive armoire, a long table and benches, and two beds flanking the fireplace, where Mrs. Huard and Josette slept. It was dark inside even on a bright day, with only one small window looking out to the yard.

The workday began early at Mrs. Huard's farm. We arose at the crack of dawn, before the rooster crowed. Antoine fed the cows and horses, cleaned the stalls, and brought in fresh hay. Mrs. Huard milked cows in the stable under the dim light of a kerosene lantern. Even Josette was up, getting ready for school. It was a long three-mile walk from the farm to the village of Savigny-le-Vieux. She had to get an early start to be there on time.

After I became acquainted with some of the workings of the farm, Mrs. Huard said that it was time for me to help. My first assignment was hauling a daily supply of firewood to the house, sweeping the ashes and starting the fire. It was harder work than it first appeared; the logs were heavy, and extricating thorny bundles of kindling wood from the wood pile was by itself a challenge. In the chill of early dawn my fingers were cold, and my body shivered. I had no gloves or warm clothing to wear, given the limited wardrobe my parents had been able to retrieve from our apartment.

After the first chores of the morning, we sat down for breakfast consisting of ersatz coffee made of brewed chicory, some homemade white bread, and pork rillettes—a country-style pâté. There were no utensils on the table. Instead Mrs. Huard and Antoine used pocketknives to eat, which incidentally served other useful functions in the course of the day. With my own pocketknife given to me by Mrs. Huard, I was ready to follow such quaint rural customs.

La Châtaigneraie, October 1942

My morning chores increased. Besides hauling firewood, I had to carry water from the well to the house for our cooking needs and fill basins with drinking water for the barnyard residents. It was a hard and tedious process to pull countless heavy pails of water from the deep recesses of the well, then lug them, two pails at a time, to the house and yard. Other chores soon followed, such as taking care of feeding pigs and rabbits and cleaning after them.

I appreciated Antoine's occasional words of encouragement noting my eagerness to do a good job, but I was disappointed that Mrs. Huard was hardly appreciative of my efforts. I had hoped that she would show me some compassion because of my young age, but she dealt with me as though I were just another hired hand. Because of Mrs. Huard's sullen personality, it was impossible to know if she was pleased or not.

Nonetheless she didn't complain, which I took to be a positive response to the way I carried out my chores. Perhaps I was too diligent, because on top of my other duties, Mrs. Huard informed me that from now on I would be responsible for taking the cows to pasture and looking after them. I felt ambivalent about my new assignment, proud that she trusted me with the herd, but wary of cows' sharp horns.

Antoine showed me how to take the cows to the pasture. He kept the herd from wandering off the trail by prodding them with a long stick, even striking some cows on the rump to keep the laggards in line. The black shepherd dog Noiraud (Blackie) followed us, happy to come along, swiftly running up and down the column and making his presence known with short barks. Antoine called the cows by their individual names, some of which obviously matched the animals' color or character. Nearing the pasture, the last maneuver I learned was sprinting ahead of the herd to open the gate wide before any cow had an opportunity to go farther along the trail.

Several lessons later I took charge of the herd. Some cows, perhaps sensing my lack of toughness, strayed from the herd. Noiraud, who kept me company, helped me bring the troublemakers back in line with threatening barks. Once in the pasture I still had to remain vigilant and keep an eye on the prancing calves determined to break away from the herd. They playfully climbed over hedgerows, trying to run away into adjacent fields. Once more Noiraud was there to give chase to the calves, catching up with them before they had a chance to escape to the other side.

I spent a good part of each day in the pasture, especially when the weather was good. The only visitor was Antoine, who came to bring my lunch—some bread, cheese and a flask of cider. Later in the day I waited for Mrs. Huard to call my name, her signal for me to go back. Surprisingly her voice carried clear across the fields, even though the pasture was a couple of hundred yards from the farm. Mrs. Huard called me "Simon," the name Mrs. Mounier gave her. It was actually the first time I used my middle name. Back home it had been "Zizi" to my family and friends; however, with gentiles, Mrs. Mounier felt that Simon was more commonplace and less likely to raise suspicion concerning my Jewish identity.

The tall hedgerows blocking my view of the countryside contributed to my feeling of isolation. I drifted into introspection, feeling blue and longing for my family. Yet I realized how fortunate we were to be still free, even though we were separated.

As I looked for some distraction to fill long hours, my pocket-knife became my life saver. I found whittling sticks of wood to be a wonderful pastime. At first my carvings were quite crude, but as my technique improved I became more creative. I was thrilled by the results and offered my nicest handiwork to Mrs. Huard and Antoine. They couldn't believe I had carved those designs with my small pocketknife. Antoine promised to find me a better one. As for Mrs. Huard, it was the first time I actually saw her smile.

Mrs. Huard owned several acres of apple trees that had to be harvested. It was the time of the year when apples were gathered to make cider. On this occasion, the Dumas and the Mauboussins, who had adjoining farms, came over with their children to help.

Prior to this get-together I had never had an opportunity to see or talk to them. Mrs. Huard must have told them who I was, because they knew my name, although they also addressed me as "Le Parisien." I was glad they were not curious about my background and that they readily accepted my presence. It was not unusual for farmers to take in foster children from cities to use as extra hands.

The orchard was near the farm. It was a spread of several acres of apple trees, a tangle of gnarled tree trunks and low branches. Most of the apples were on the ground. We spread out across the orchard, filling our baskets with every apple in sight, regardless if it was perfect or rotten, since they were to be pressed for cider. The squashed apples gave out an intoxicating sweet and pungent smell that saturated the air. It was a long and tedious process, gathering and unloading each basket of apples into a horsewagon Antoine brought to the site. Several days later, most of the apples were brought to the cider shed, pressed into a thick mash, the juice then extracted and funnelled into barrels.

After the harvest Mrs. Huard treated her neighbors with a roasted piglet and fixings. She also brought out for the occasion some of her best bottles of her homemade "Calvados," an apple brandy that quickly vanished. Everyone was in a jovial mood, even Mrs. Huard, her face flushed and giddy like a young girl.

7

La Châtaigneraie, November 1942
Since arriving in Savigny-le-Vieux, I had few opportunities to see my sister, despite the close proximity of our locations. I missed her a lot and couldn't wait to share with her all of the events of the past couple of months. Mrs. Huard was hardly sympathetic to my pleas to take time off from my chores to see her. She eventually relented and grudgingly gave me her permission. I flew more than walked to Alleray. The prospect of seeing my sister gave me wings.

It was amazing how quickly our lives had changed since we left Vincennes. I found Alice in the stable helping Mrs. Ledauphin milk the cows. My sister already could have passed as a farm girl, with her cheeks rosy from outdoor work. We hugged and laughed, thrilled to be together again. Mrs. Ledauphin greeted me, cheerful as always. In that moment my feelings of loneliness from the past months vanished, my spirits soaring. Alice and I managed to spend some time alone while she went about the farm taking care of her chores.

In many ways my sister's life on the farm was similar to mine. She worked long hours performing many tasks, some more difficult than others. But she only had nice words for everyone, especially for Mrs. Ledauphin, who had taken her under her wing and made her feel she was a part of her family. She was fond of Solange, who kept her company, and of the little Wilfrid, who reminded her so much of Michel. While listening to my sister's happy comments I didn't have the heart to dispel her good spirits by complaining about Mrs. Huard. Instead I painted a bright picture to make her believe everything was just fine. Such occasional visits with Alice always seemed far too short, yet the pleasure lingered on long afterward.

After supper Mrs. Huard led us in evening prayers. It was a ritual I had followed since I arrived, not wanting to raise questions about my religious background. Josette, Antoine and I knelt beside Mrs. Huard on the hard dirt floor, facing a cross hanging over the fireplace. I became panicky when Mrs. Huard handed me a *chapelet* (rosary) for the first time. I furtively watched the others, mimicking their gestures, joining both hands in front of my chest and keeping my head bowed, mumbling words under my breath in unison with their voices. I felt terribly nervous, hoping my deception would work. I listened carefully, trying to memorize the prayers, but they recited them too quickly for me to have a chance to learn them.

By chance I noticed that Mrs. Huard kept a small prayer book in her sewing basket. With some trepidation I borrowed it, hoping she wouldn't look for it. I took the prayer book tucked under my shirt to the pasture, where I leisurely memorized the prayers. "Pater Noster" and "Ave Maria," practicing every single word out loud until I was able to recite them without hesitation. Thereafter I confidently joined in with the others no longer whispering the words, to make sure that Mrs. Huard noticed.

My indoctrination into the Catholic religion continued every Sunday, when Mrs. Huard, Josette and I attended Mass at the church of Savigny-le-Vieux. There was a social event, an opportunity for farmers of the area to congregate after Mass, at the local café. For this weekly occasion Mrs. Huard and Josette wore their finest clothes and wide-brimmed hats. We were not about to walk to the village all dressed up, so instead we rode in a cart, joined by other local farmers also on their way to church. The small village square was noisy, filled with carts and horses and a crowd waiting outside on the front steps before Mass started. People wore mostly dark colors, shades of blacks and grays matching the weathered stones of the old church.

On my first Sunday in church I imagined everybody was looking at me, watching my every move in order to catch me making a mistake. It was a fear that happily would never be realized. I eventually learned the rituals, in order to act like a devout Christian. Upon entering the church, I never forgot to cross myself with holy water. Sitting next to Mrs. Huard and Josette in the pew, I made sure to follow each one of their responses to the priest's Latin incantations, chanting "amens" when they did. I kneeled, bowed and prayed in unison with them.

Because my parents had had no affiliation with a synagogue, had never prayed at home or celebrated Jewish holidays, I had grown up without any notion of or belief in a supreme being. The concept that people prayed to a god was strange to me. However, being surrounded by the elaborate trappings of the church and rituals made me ponder for the first time if indeed there could be a supreme being who ruled people's lives and the universe. If there was a god, was he Catholic or Jewish or both, I wondered?

Nonetheless, I couldn't help but be fascinated by the pomp and solemnity of Mass, as the priest and altar boys, in fancy robes trimmed with gold, led the faithful in prayer. I was also fascinated by the dramatic architecture, from the graceful ceiling arches soaring high above, to the decorative stained-glass windows, casting splashes of colors upon the statues of saints lining the aisles.

When the weather turned colder and frost blanketed the ground, I no longer had to take the cows to pasture. It was a welcome respite. However, Mrs. Huard made sure I remained busy. Splitting logs for the fireplace was my newest chore, in order to free Antoine for other tasks. I had watched him before from afar, lifting and swinging his axe as easily as he swatted pesky flies. But this time I had to pay closer attention to his technique, which consisted of standing a log up on a tree stump and, with a quick motion swinging the axe down the middle, slicing the wood seemingly effortlessly. Within minutes a large pile of split wood lay on the ground.

I envied Antoine's strength and bulging muscles, and was aware of my skinny arms, hardly a match for such a task. My first attempts were dismal. Just lifting the long-handle axe was a supreme effort. After countless tries, I managed to find a way to split logs; however I was slow compared to Antoine. Every so often I rolled up my sleeves to check my arms, hoping to find I already had biceps like his. It was, of course, only wishful thinking, but I continued the task at hand until I had split enough wood to last for a week.

I thought Mrs. Huard would be satisfied that I had enough work, but she was not. I never complained, and perhaps it was my fault that she gave me more and more chores. It didn't occur to me to refuse her requests. I was somewhat afraid she would lash out at me, causing problems that could jeopardize my stay. So I obediently went about performing my next task, which was making butter from cream.

The procedure was brand new to me. But like most work on the farm, it was not terribly complicated; it only required strength and patience. Mrs. Huard kept a butter churn in a space adjoining the stable. She made butter once a week from heavy cream collected in tall jars. The butter churn was a barrel-shaped wooden box, mounted on a stand, with a crank on its side. Mrs. Huard poured cream inside through a small opening. I then continuously rotated the churn until the cream finally coagulated into butter. It was a long and tedious procedure that made my arm painfully sore.

My life with Mrs. Huard was not a happy one. I was overworked and treated like a servant. I yearned for some appreciation from her, but it never came. While I was sometimes miserable, I couldn't overlook the fact that I never went to bed hungry. In this respect I was fortunate to live on a farm where no one needed ration coupons to survive. All the food we ate was home grown, and there always an ample supply of poultry, pork and dairy products on hand. Mrs. Huard made her own bread. I helped her knead the dough and shape it into large round loaves, which were baked outdoors in a brick oven.

Lunch was the main meal of the day, with the ever-present pork, bread and boiled potatoes. At times there were some variations like a chicken or a *pot-au-feu* (stew). Mrs. Huard and Antoine enjoyed a fermented cider that quickly went to my head if I had too many glasses. It was my job to fill the pitcher from a barrel. Because there was no spigot to pour the cider, it had to be siphoned out. The procedure consisted of removing the cork from the top of the barrel, then inserting a length of rubber hose into the opening and sucking the air to force the liquid up. I invariably swallowed a mouthful of cider before I could start pouring into the pitcher.

I was at Mrs. Huard's beck and call whenever she needed me. My natural squeamishness was put to the test whenever she killed a chicken for our next meal. Because she used the blood for gravy, she made me stand by her side with a cup. Once she settled on a chicken, she twisted the neck of her victim, and with a sharp knife removed one of the eyeballs. I held the cup beneath the chicken to collect the blood gushing out.

There were other instances when I had to look the other way, filled with revulsion. Once I took part in the slaughter of a pig, holding him down even though his legs were tied, while Antoine slit his throat. The pitiful squealing haunted me in my sleep. In spite of my disgust for these chores, I was aware that neither Mrs. Huard nor Antoine was cruel or sadistic, only killing to feed all of us.

La Châtaigneraie, January 1943
Winter held the countryside firmly in its frozen grip. I dreaded going out at the crack of dawn for my first chores of the morning. I had to haul heavy logs to the house and pull kindling from the frost-covered wood pile, then fetch water from the well, dragging pails of water across the yard and at times falling on the icy ground.

The cold air felt like an invisible frozen shroud coiling itself tightly around my body. My ears tingled and my toes were numb, but worst of all, my fingers remained stiff and blue until I could revive them at the fireplace. I looked back with nostalgia to past winters at home, when I had hardly been aware of the harshness of the cold weather. City streets were more sheltered from the wind than the open countryside. I had been outside only for brief periods of time, going to school or running errands for my mother. I had taken for granted my warm clothing that shielded me from the cold, and I missed the coat, gloves and socks that I no longer had.

Soon after I arrived at the farm I had traded my only pair of shoes, quite worn and outgrown, for an old pair of sabots (wooden clogs) that Mrs. Huard had saved. Every farmer I'd seen wore them. Unfortunately the clogs she gave me were too large for my feet. I stuffed them with straw to keep my bare feet from slipping out, because my last pair of socks was in tatters. Clogs, to be sure, were more practical to wear than shoes, especially on muddy trails or in the stable, where cow manure was always underfoot. But it took me a lot longer that I had expected to get used to them. Besides, the clogs were heavy, and the uneven, rough-hewn wood rubbed and chafed my toes.

The barn where I slept offered little protection against the penetrating cold, especially when howling frigid winds found their way inside through cracks in the doors and siding.

I slept with Antoine, and in the close confines of the bed, his body kept me warmer. I occasionally felt his muscular body pressed against mine during the night. I didn't give it further thought, because we both moved in our sleep and the bed was quite narrow. When I occasionally felt his arm across my chest I managed to wiggle out and push it away without waking him up. But then one night I was jolted from my sleep by Antoine's calloused hands groping my body. I pulled away from his reach, suddenly afraid, perhaps instinctively sensing the sexual implications of his touch and thinking it wrong. I don't know for sure what it was that made me react so nervously, because even though I'd just turned thirteen, I was terribly naive.

My parents had kept mum about such topics, and the books I'd read and movies I'd seen in the past had never revealed or hinted at sexuality. Whatever I had learned about sex was from my schoolmates, who, like me, were ill-informed. As for homosexuality, I had no idea it existed; the word was not even a part of my vocabulary. I might have forgotten this incident, but Antoine made other attempts to touch me, even intimately. I pushed him away, but I became panicky when he became bolder and more persistent. What could I do to make him stop without making him angry I wondered?

Out of sheer desperation I pleaded with Mrs. Huard to find me another place to sleep, saying that I was shivering at night from the bitter cold and felt ill. I didn't think that she would believe such a blatant lie, but I couldn't have told her the truth. Mrs. Huard listened to me, examining me with her probing small round eyes as though she was evaluating how sick I was. She didn't give me a clue about the way she felt.

To my astonishment, several days later she told me that she had come to a decision: Josette would give me her bed, while Mrs. Huard and her daughter would sleep together. Was it possible that Mrs. Huard had a heart after all, or was she only worried that I might be unable to work anymore? Whatever her true motives were, I was thrilled to move into the farmhouse and sleep under a thick down-filled quilt.

I was concerned that Antoine would realize why I had moved, and afraid he might become hostile and make my life difficult. However, he never let on if he knew and, as in the past, remained friendly with me.

La Châtaigneraie, February 1943

I visited my sister on her fifteenth birthday. It had snowed during the night. The countryside was a picture postcard landscape, with thick fluffy cotton balls clinging to tree branches and cow trails blurred under a coating of white powder. When I arrived at the Ledauphin's farm, a man I'd never seen before was in the courtyard, busy hitching a horse to a wagon. The stranger acknowledged my presence with a smile and saluted me, tipping the brim of his cap with his index finger. I assumed he was a helpful neighbor who had come over to lend a hand to Mrs. Ledauphin.

I went to the farmhouse and found Mrs. Ledauphin and Alice inside, attending to some chores. Mrs. Ledauphin burst out with joy when she saw me, exclaiming "Marcel is back!" For a split second I was at a loss, until I remembered Marcel was her husband's name, then I realized that the man in the courtyard was Mr. Ledauphin. Such wonderful news! I was happy for her and her children's good fortune, thinking that Providence had seen to reward her for her good heart.

I learned that Mr. Ledauphin was one of the few lucky prisoners from his camp who had been liberated from Germany only a couple of days before. He was already hard at work on his farm. We celebrated Alice's birthday and Mr. Ledauphin's homecoming by gathering for lunch with Mr. Ledauphin at the head of the table. He struck me as a nice man, friendly-looking, with a twinkle in his eyes and, like his wife, a sunny disposition. Watching his children's happy faces, I couldn't help but feeling envious that they had parents watching over them.

Alice said that she had not heard from Mrs. Mounier or from the Bonneaus. I was disappointed and worried. Almost five months had elapsed without a word. I recalled Mrs. Mounier promising she would stay in touch with us and return. Had she run into trouble helping other Jewish children, we wondered?

La Châtaigneraie, March 1943

Since coming to Savigny-le-Vieux I had been without news from the outside world. At times it felt as though the war was a figment of my imagination. There was no local newspaper and Mrs. Huard didn't own a radio, and even if she had had one, there was no electricity. As a result we depended solely on rumors for news, which failed to give us much comfort. The only reminder of the occupation was an occasional German military convoy passing through the village, but no soldiers were ever seen nearby. In this respect I was fortunate to be hidden in such a remote location.

I had almost given up on seeing Mrs. Mounier again, when one day she unexpectedly arrived. The dogs alerted us that we had company. I came out of the stable and saw her with Mrs. Ledauphin, stepping down from the cart into the courtyard. I ran up to them excitedly. Mrs. Mounier looked even prettier than I remembered, with her blond hair framing her smiling face. She was wearing a winter coat trimmed with a fur collar, and looked like a fairytale princess descending from her royal carriage. I must have been caught under her spell, because she laughingly said, "Has the cat got your tongue?" Then she hugged me close to her, the perfume she wore overwhelming my senses.

Mrs. Mounier took me aside while Mrs. Huard and Mrs. Ledauphin chatted. I told her I was anxious to know if she had any news about my parents and my brother. She assured me that Michel was in good health and happy with the Leclères; but she didn't have such good news regarding my parents. She hesitated before she said that my parents had been arrested, her voice almost a whisper, as though she was trying to soften the impact of her words. I froze in a state of shock, my mind reeling. She wrapped her arms around me, holding me tight. My heart ached and tears welled in my eyes, but somehow I managed not to cry, aware that Mrs. Huard or Mrs. Ledauphin might ask questions.

Mrs. Mounier briefly related what she'd heard from the Bonneaus. Last summer they received word from my parents that they were prisoners in Drancy, the internment camp where Jews were held before being deported. Madeleine Bonneau had gone to see them and brought them food. She learned how they had been betrayed trying to cross the demarcation line and arrested before they were able to reach the "non-occupied zone." They hadn't had a chance because the Frenchman they had trusted to guide them to safety had pocketed the money and delivered them to German border guards. From there they had been sent back north and incarcerated in Drancy.

For a while the Bonneaus had received permission to visit them, until the French police who ran the camp denied any further visits. Mrs. Mounier said that since that time the Bonneaus had had no word of their whereabouts. Seeing how sad I looked, she tried cheering me up by saying she'd heard that in the past some Jewish prisoners had been released from Drancy. "It could happen to your parents and to their friends" she said earnestly, her voice sounding hopeful, as though she really believed that such a miracle could take place.

Making sure that she couldn't be heard by Mrs. Huard, Mrs. Mounier asked me if I was treated well. I was hesitant to tell her how I really felt, thinking I had no right to complain while my parents and their friends were held captive behind barbed wires. She must have noticed my reluctance, because she insisted upon knowing the whole truth. I conceded that I worked hard and at times was lonely, without blaming Mrs. Huard, who was the cause of my unhappiness. Nonetheless Mrs. Mounier guessed the truth. She whispered in my ear that she would try to relocate me in Savigny-le-Vieux, if that was my wish. I nodded, willing to take a chance with another guardian.

Mrs. Mounier promised to return soon. After she left I thought about my parents, closing my eyes to better conjure up their faces. They seemed to be looking at me, their expressions serene, without a hint of fear. Were they sending me a message from afar, not to give up hope and to take heart?

La Châtaigneraie, April 1943

The snow reluctantly melted away, revealing green patches under the frosty white meadows. The cool air smelled sweet from the tree buds heeding the early spring stirrings. I was grateful to have endured the bitter winter months without catching a cold or becoming ill, despite Mrs. Huard's sarcastic assessment that "Parisian boys are not cut out for living on a farm."

I didn't take her remark to heart, sensing that she secretly appreciated my diligence in carrying out all the chores she had heaped upon me. I had never asked her for a favor, except when I had pleaded to move out of the barn, and that was not for the reason she'd imagined. Meanwhile I was enjoying the benefit of sleeping in the farmhouse by the side of the fireplace's glowing embers, and I no longer suffered from the cold now that I was under the thick quilt filled with goose feathers.

Since moving into the farmhouse I had had opportunities to observe Josette when she did her homework; most of the time she was fretting, chewing on her pencil and nagging her mother for help. Once Mrs. Huard was so irritated by her constant whining that she flew into a terrible rage. I waited for the storm to pass, then proposed helping Josette with her homework in exchange for giving up some of my chores. Mrs. Huard, to my surprise, readily accepted my offer. Although Josette was about eleven years old, her learning skills were more like those of a second-grader. She was also lazy and spoiled. I suddenly realized that I had quite a challenge ahead of me. I took my tutoring seriously, determined to keep my end of the bargain.

Fortunately Josette listened to me and made some progress, solving simple arithmetic problems and learning how to write compositions. Actually, I was enjoying my role and was proud that I could motivate Josette to learn. I was shocked when Mrs. Huard actually thanked me for helping her daughter.

8

Savigny-le-Vieux, April 1943

One day I saw from afar a horsedrawn cart approaching our farm. My heart beat faster when I recognized Mrs. Ledauphin holding the reins and Mrs. Mounier sitting next to her. I ran up to greet them. I had never expected Mrs. Mounier to return so soon, especially not with the news that she had found another home for me in the village of Savigny-le-Vieux. Before I had recovered from my surprise, Mrs. Mounier told me she had already made all the necessary arrangements for me to leave at once.

Still reeling from the shock, I quickly gathered my few belongings and waited in the courtyard to depart. I had dreamt of such a moment for a long time, and now that it had arrived I felt nervous, as though some unexpected event might interfere and spoil that happy moment.

Mrs. Huard was quite upset when she learned I was leaving. Nonetheless, our goodbyes were friendly. Mrs. Huard even hugged me, her usual stern expression softened by a smile. Josette kissed me, and Antoine squeezed my hand in his strong grip, wishing me *"bonne chance!"* I climbed into the cart next to Mrs. Mounier and we left, Mrs. Ledauphin guiding her horse toward the trail ahead. I turned back for a last glimpse at Mrs. Huard, Josette and Antoine still standing there.

While riding to the village, Mrs. Mounier said she had not expected to find another place for me so quickly. By a stroke of luck, someone in the village had been looking for a boarder, preferably an older boy able to help with light chores. Her name was Mrs. Prim, an elderly widow with two children already in her care. Mrs. Mounier told me that Mrs. Prim had seemed to be a kind and caring woman. "I believe you will be happier with her than with Mrs. Huard," she said confidently, her warm smile making me agree.

Meanwhile we arrived in the village square. Mrs. Ledauphin remained in her cart while I walked with Mrs. Mounier to my future home. A couple of hundred feet from the square we came upon a tiny whitewashed house standing near the church's main entrance. I suddenly realized that I had seen this humble shack before on my way to Mass, without paying much attention to it. Mrs. Prim was waiting outside on the doorstep with two children gawking at us with undisguised curiosity.

She cheerfully waved us inside the dimly lit interior. It was crowded with furniture, and a stale smell of food, burnt wood and ashes still lingered in the air. We sat at a table while Mrs. Prim served us cider and introduced us to the children, a sister and brother. Annette, about ten years old, was slender, with a mop of dark curly hair framing her narrow face and alert probing eyes. Her younger brother, Maurice, was about seven, and in contrast to his sister he was quite chubby, with a large forehead, short straw-colored hair and pale blue watery eyes. I never would have guessed they were related. Mrs. Mounier had not said much about them except that they were refugees from Paris. It suddenly occurred to me that they might be Jewish, and I wondered if Mrs. Mounier knew more about them than she cared to share with me.

I turned my attention to Mrs. Prim, a heavyset woman with a double chin but pretty features, who wore her white hair tied in a bun. At first glance she looked as if she were in her sixties, yet upon further scrutiny, her unlined, youthful-looking face suggested she might be a lot younger.

The walls were barren except for sepia photographs on each side of the fireplace. Mrs. Mounier inquired about one of them, a portrait of a young-looking soldier wearing a French uniform. *"C'est Gustave, mon fils"* (It's Gustave, my son), replied Mrs. Prim. She was eager to talk to us about her son, who had been captured by the Germans during the summer of 1940, and since then had been held in a prisoner-of-war camp. Mrs. Prim glanced at a cross hanging on the wall: "I pray every day to the good Lord for his safe return," she said, reverently crossing herself.

She reached for a tin box on the mantelpiece, from which she took out a slim packet of letters, which she waved in front of Mrs. Mounier. "Can you possibly imagine, *chère madame*, that this is the only mail I've received from my son since he became a prisoner!" she lamented. Mrs. Prim then complained about how she struggled to make ends meet, taking Mrs. Mounier in her confidence: "It's not easy for an older woman to get by, especially since my husband passed away." She pointed to her wedding picture, in which she was a smiling, slender bride next to a serious-looking groom with an impressive handlebar mustache. Mrs. Prim gazed fondly at the photograph, reminiscing about her husband.

Finally Mrs. Mounier said she had to leave. I accompanied her back to the cart, where Mrs. Ledauphin had been waiting. On the way there she gave me some last-minute instructions, urging me to do my best to be helpful and to get along with Mrs. Prim. She hugged me and promised to return soon. I should have been buoyed by her visit, yet when she was gone I felt a tinge of sadness, already missing her good humor and the affection that she'd showered upon me during her brief visit.

Savigny-le-Vieux, May 1943

I quickly had to adapt myself to living in a tiny house crammed full with beds and furniture. It was quite a dramatic change from living in a farm surrounded by wide-open vistas, but otherwise I found the same primitive conditions existing in Mrs. Prim's house. Without electricity, running water or plumbing, Mrs. Prim made do with a well and an outhouse. Annette showed me the way to where they were located, down a flight of crooked steps leading to a backyard overrun with weeds and thorny vines. Annette then took me to the cellar, a dank room lined with cobwebs, where Mrs. Prim kept a barrel of cider and potatoes, onions and some other food stored in a wooden chest.

I noticed that Mrs. Prim used a cane whenever she stepped outside, and sometimes inside the house. It made me curious because she looked healthy and robust. Annette confided that she had heard Mrs. Prim mentioning that she suffered from arthritis. However neither one of us had any clear idea about the nature of that crippling condition.

Suffice to say, at times the pain made Mrs. Prim irritable and short-tempered. With such a handicap she was incapable of carrying heavy loads, such as pails of water or firewood. As a result, those chores fell on Annette's frail shoulders. I could scarcely imagine how she had managed to do such hard work before I came.

As soon as I was settled I took over those demanding tasks. By then I was already used to hard physical work, and such chores were no longer a struggle for me. Besides, I was eager to please Mrs. Prim. I volunteered to handle the myriad daily chores, keeping the fire going and cleaning the ashes, tidy up the house and helping her prepare meals. She occasionally sent me to a nearby farm to replenish the food supply, which I found to be a happy diversion.

Such errands gave me an opportunity to escape for a little while from my confining surroundings. On the way I wandered through the village, enjoying my new-found freedom. The village of Savigny-le-Vieux was not particularly picturesque, but its weathered stone houses capped with steep slate roofs and tall chimneys had a rustic charm.

The hub of the village was the church, standing tall in the middle of the square next to a monument commemorating the fallen soldiers of World War I. It was a sight I had encountered many times while crossing France with my father and sister during the exodus of 1940. The monument was a constant reminder of the sacrifice of Frenchmen who had died on the battlefield. The church rose above a bluff ringed by a stone wall, and below, a cobblestone area served as parking space for farmers attending Sunday Mass. Across the way, on the other side of the narrow county road, a row of two-story stone dwellings stretched along several blocks. The village had a café, which was always well patronized, and a few stores including a bakery, a butcher, a clogmaker and a blacksmith.

When I didn't have to hurry back, I enjoyed stopping in front of the shop of *"le sabotier,"* (the clogmaker). I would stand with my nose pressed against the glass, attempting to catch a glimpse of Mr. Lemaitre at work surrounded by stacks of wooden blocks and finished clogs. Mr. Lemaitre was a portly man who wore a cap and a leather apron covered with sawdust, and he usually had a cigarette butt clinging to his lower lip. He eventually took notice of me, and stuck his head outside the door to find out what I wanted. I told him how much I enjoyed watching him work, hoping he was not angry with me for disturbing him. Instead of being annoyed at my intrusion, with a friendly grin and a wave of his hand he invited me to come inside, cautioning me to stay away from flying chips. He began the process by selecting various chisels from his workbench; then, mallet in hand, he quickly chipped away golden ribbons of wood until the rough-hewn block of wood cradled in his lap emerged as a perfectly shaped clog. Mr. Lemaitre was simply amazing!

I was equally fascinated watching Mr. Voisin, who was the village *"forgeron"* (blacksmith). His shop was at the other end of the village, where farmers often could be seen in the street waiting their turns with their horses in tow. Through the open double doors of his shop it was easy to spot Mr. Voisin, even from afar, his burly silhouette leaning over an anvil in a shower of orange and white sparks. The best time, though, to watch him ply his trade was when he was in the process of nailing a horseshoe in place with powerful taps while his helper held the horse still by plying it with handfuls of oats.

I thought it was unusual for a small village such as Savigny-le-Vieux to have two elementary schools. Nonetheless, Annette went to the girls' school located in the village hall, while Maurice attended the boys' school in his teacher's home. I noticed that after school Annette diligently took care of her homework while her brother hardly opened his notebooks. Not unexpectedly, as a result of his poor grades Maurice's teacher sent word to Mrs. Prim to come to the school to discuss the problem. However, a flare-up of arthritis that kept Mrs. Prim practically bedridden prevented her from walking even that short distance. I was flattered when she asked me to meet on her behalf with Mr. Crochet, the teacher, to handle such a delicate matter.

Mrs. Prim's misfortune was my good luck. Mr. Crochet was a jovial, young-looking man with an alert expression. After I explained why I had come instead of Mrs. Prim, he said he knew at once from the way I expressed myself that I couldn't possibly be a local boy. He was curious and prodded me with questions. I didn't want to say too much, knowing it was best to keep my story simple in order not to arouse suspicion about my Jewish identity. I simply said that I was a refugee from Paris in the care of Mrs. Prim.

Mr. Crochet seemed to enjoy our conversation. He showed me around the front room of his house, which was used as a classroom. A lingering smell of ink brought back memories of my school days in Montreuil. This improvised classroom was cluttered with small wooden desks, assorted stools, chairs and bookcases lining the back wall. I commented on the novels I'd read in the past, saying that since coming to Savigny-le-Vieux I missed having had books to read most of all. I was too shy to ask him if I could borrow a book. However, as though he had read my mind, Mr. Crochet selected several books and handed them to me. "I have an entire library at your disposal" he said with a wink. I couldn't believe my sudden good fortune, clutching my newfound treasures with delight against my chest.

A calender next to the blackboard caught my eye because of the reproduction of a painting depicting farmers gathered in a field at sunset, their heads bowed in a silent prayer. I remembered having seen it before in my Larousse dictionary. I was trying to impress Mr. Crochet with my knowledge when I remarked that it was *"l' Angelus"* by Millet. I also mentioned that memorizing famous paintings had been one of the games my older sister and I had played at home. I wistfully said that to draw again would be my greatest pleasure.

My revelation prompted Mr. Crochet to leave the room and return with a small package wrapped in yellowed newspapers. *"Voila un petit cadeau pour toi"* (Here is a little present for you), he said rather mysteriously. Then he urged me: "Go ahead, open it up!" I untied the string that held together the wrapping and discovered inside a sketch pad and a flat black metal box. Lifting the lid, I gazed upon a watercolor set with an assortment of fine brushes. I was speechless, overcome by such a wonderful gift. Mr. Crochet's voice brought me back to earth. He proceeded to tell me that a late uncle who had dabbled in art had given it to him many years ago. He patted me affectionately on my back, saying: "I have a hunch that you will put it to better use than Tonton ever did!"

I thanked him profusely and promised that I would help Maurice with his homework. Later I thought that the best way to show Mr. Crochet my appreciation would be to draw something special for him. The old church seemed a perfect subject for my first attempt, especially since I had a perfect vantage point from Mrs. Prim's house.

I sat on the front steps of the house with my sketch pad on my knees, pencil in hand, the watercolors and brushes next to me. I savored this special moment, feeling my pulse racing from both nervousness and exhilaration at the thought of drawing once again. Annette and Maurice kept me company, curiously looking over my shoulder, awaiting my next move.

At first I was tentative in sketching the outline of the church, afraid of wasting the precious sheet of paper in front of me. However, as my drawing took shape, my confidence soared, and I became immersed in the creative process. When the drawing was completed, I gingerly proceeded to experiment with watercolors. It was the first time I had ever used the medium. To my delight the bell tower's weathered stones came alive with deftly placed strokes of bluish gray and touches of moss green. Blends of light blue and mauve suggested the sky above. I was rewarded for my first attempt by loud clapping from my two young critics. The noise drew Mrs. Prim out from inside the house. She held my drawing at arms length: *"C'est très joli!"* (It's very nice), she said approvingly. But the final verdict was yet to come. I delivered the sketch to Mr. Crochet, awaiting his reaction with trepidation. His face lit up as he examined my watercolor. "Tonton would be proud of you!" he exclaimed.

From the house I had a front-row seat to watch parishioners come to church. During the week there was a mere trickle of faithful coming to worship, mostly elderly women slowly making their way up the front steps.

But the busiest time was on Sunday, when farmers' families flocked to church. For her part Mrs. Prim hardly ever attended Mass, nor did she pray at home as Mrs. Huard did. Perhaps this was because of her arthritis, which prevented her from kneeling. Nonetheless, when she opted to pray I readily joined her to enforce the pretense that I was Christian. As for Annette and Maurice, they didn't seem to know the prayers, confirming my suspicion that they were Jewish.

From the first time I entered the church I had been fascinated by its architecture, its colorful stained-glass windows and its gilded statues. Occasionally, when no one was in sight, I ventured inside with my drawing pad to sketch the saints standing high above on narrow stone ledges. It occurred to me that it might be sacrilegious to draw pictures in a church, so I was ready at a moment's notice to hide my sketch pad under my shirt if parishioners should walk in.

Despite my alertness the village priest, Father Perrin, caught me. I was so absorbed I didn't hear his footsteps. By the time I saw him shuffling down the aisle it was too late to hide my sketch pad or pretend I had come in to pray. I expected to be admonished. Much to my relief, however, the rotund Father Perrin greeted me warmly: "I am glad to finally meet one of the little Parisians staying with Mrs. Prim." He had obviously seen me before. Then he examined my drawings, saying "You have a wonderful talent my lad, it's a gift from God!"

I was thrilled that Mrs. Prim had given me permission to spend the day with my sister. I had not seen Alice since moving to Savigny-le-Vieux and was anxious to share all the latest happenings with her. There was so much to tell her, especially about my good fortune in having met Mr. Crochet and about the wonderful books I'd read, and I also wanted to show her my drawings.

When I arrived at the Ledauphin's farm Alice acted rather mysteriously, keeping me in suspense until she brought out a girl's bicycle from the barn. "It's mine!" she happily exclaimed. "Don't you remember it?" I nodded, yet was at a loss, because while I recognized her bicycle with the familiar coat of blue paint and gold trim, I still couldn't figure out how she had gotten hold of it. My sister toyed with me for a while until she decided to clear up the mystery. Her bicycle had been retrieved after the roundup and kept in storage with the Bonneaus.

During Mrs. Mounier's last visit Alice had given her a message asking the Bonneaus for a special favor, namely, to ship her bike to

Savigny-le-Vieux. She said she was shocked when it arrived, because she had not expected the Bonneaus to go to the trouble and expense.

As usual Alice and I reviewed events since our last get-together, but somehow neither one of us was able to bring up the topic of our parents' arrest. I suspected that my sister, like me, couldn't summon the courage to share with me the tragic news Mrs. Mounier had told her. We kept our pain from each other, locked in our hearts.

9

La Renouardière, June 1943

The first couple of months I spent with Mrs. Prim were a vast improvement over my stay with Mrs. Huard. This was mostly because I was not as overworked and because reading and drawing lifted my spirits whenever I felt low. While I was generally happier than with Mrs. Huard, food was not as plentiful as on the farm, and at times the crowded house made life stressful for everyone. I could often feel tension and raw nerves.

Mrs. Prim appeared kind and gentle at first. But my initial impression was dispelled when I discovered that she could often be mean-spirited and even cruel, especially toward young Maurice. On occasions when he didn't respond at once to her commands, Mrs. Prim struck him on the head with her cane while cursing him for being slow, stupid and pig-headed. I was distressed to witness such harsh punishment, but was powerless to interfere.

As for me, being older and more mature, I was able to keep on her good side, toeing the line and not giving her any reason for getting angry. However, to be fair to Mrs. Prim, she was not a monster, nor for that matter were Annette and Maurice angels. Like all young children, at times they were downright obnoxious and irritating. It was inevitable that in such cramped quarters Mrs. Prim's patience was often pushed to the limit. There seemed to be no possible solution to the overcrowding.

Some time later, however, Mrs. Prim gleefully made a startling announcement. She said that soon we would move to a larger house in the hamlet of La Renouardière. I was quite familiar with La Renouardière, which was located about half a mile from the village at the end of a dirt trail that cut through apple orchards.

At first I assumed it was merely a coincidence that this house was next door to the Geslins, the kind farmers who regularly supplied us with dairy products and poultry. I later learned it was hardly a coincidence, because Mrs. Prim was a distant relation of the Geslins, who owned the property.

Judging from the conditions in which we lived and by the way Mrs. Prim often complained about how poor she was, I couldn't imagine how she could have afforded to pay the rent, much less buy such a house. The Geslins, father and son, helped move Mrs. Prim's furniture with their horse-drawn wagon.

It was a thrill to move into our new home. The house was in good repair, a brick-and-stone structure with a cheerful-looking red-tiled roof and green shutters. The modest-size house was a princely residence in my eyes, at least compared to the matchbox we'd just left. Still, there was no running water or electricity, and the interior was no more than a traditional one-room house with a dirt floor, beamed ceiling and a fireplace. But there was more than ample room for beds and furnishings, with extra space in an attic and in another storage room connected by a side door.

The hamlet of La Renouardière consisted of the Geslins' and the Bertrands' farms—a jumble of sheds, barns, stables and yards populated with noisy feathered tenants. I had yet to meet the Bertrands, but I was already acquainted with *"Père et Mère Geslin"* (Father and Mother Geslin), as they liked to be addressed. They were in their early forties, both short, with weather-beaten ruddy faces and calloused hands. The twinkle in Père Geslin's eyes hinted at his humorous nature, while his wife looked more reserved. I'd briefly met their teenage son and daughter, who worked alongside them. Roland was eighteen, short and stocky like his parents. His younger sister, Thérèse, was about my age, pert-looking, with high cheek bones and gray eyes. She shyly responded to my greetings with a smile whenever she saw me.

I liked the Geslins very much because of their friendly ways. Every so often, after I was through with my daily chores, I went over to their farm to help and to escape the tedium of my daily life. It also gave me an opportunity to talk to someone besides Mrs. Prim and the children. I sensed that Père and Mère Geslin appreciated my eagerness and zeal—particularly Père Geslin, who was intrigued by my lively conversation and vocabulary. He often teased me: *"T'as la langue bien pendue, comme un vrai Parisien!"* (You have a glib tongue, like a true Parisian!). I chose to think that he meant it as a compliment.

I was not asked by the Geslins to do any specific chores, but if they needed an extra hand I was happy to pitch in. I began spending more time with them, but I never neglected my chores. I enjoyed going to the fields in a horse-drawn wagon. I even tried riding atop one of their huge draft horses without a saddle, holding on to the collar harness. It was both scary and exhilarating. Whenever I ate with the family, Père Geslin rambled on between mouthfuls of food and swigs of cider. He was quite opinionated, and unlike most farmers I'd met, who were usually closed-mouthed, he freely expressed his opinion about any topic, including religion and politics.

He was against every institution. As far as he was concerned, the government and the church had too much power and were meddling in everybody's life. I gathered that Mère Geslin did not see eye to eye with him, especially when he spoke disparagingly of the church and religion. But she kept quiet, ignoring his lack of piety, at least in front of her children. Père Geslin often teased his wife, saying that since he was such a sinner, he hoped that she prayed to God to save his soul.

Politics was another topic he relished. He claimed that General de Gaulle was the only French hero remaining after the debacle of 1940. "He is a true patriot, not like this scum Marshal Pétain, a traitor who sold out France to the enemy" was his conclusion. He called the Nazis *doryphores*, the destructive beetles who devoured potato crops.

I was surprised and impressed to learn that Père Geslin had a short-wave radio that he kept hidden in the barn because it was illegal to own one. I would never have guessed that a plain farmer like him would have such sophisticated and modern electronic equipment and the know-how to operate it. Père Geslin, true to his character, enjoyed thumbing his nose at the Germans. Such an infraction would have cost him dearly if a collaborator had gotten wind that he owned a short-wave radio and denounced him. He could have been arrested and suffered dire consequences. Despite the danger and the frequent jamming of the airwaves, he persisted in tuning in, and was occasionally rewarded by tuning in a French-speaking broadcast beamed from London.

For the first time since coming to Savigny-le-Vieux I had a glimmer of the events taking place in France and elsewhere in Europe. Père Geslin gleefully said that the despised "beetles" were finally getting a taste of their own medicine. I listened with rapt attention as he told us what he heard on the radio. The Nazi forces apparently were no longer able to crush the Soviets at will. For the first time since they invaded Russia, they had lost a crucial battle at Stalingrad and had been forced to retreat with enormous losses.

They had also been beaten by Allied forces in North Africa. Even in France, despite harsh reprisals, partisans routinely sabotaged Nazi military installations and ambushed troops. Those reports sounded almost too good to be true, but Père Geslin was convinced the Allies would never spread lies and propaganda like the Nazis.

The Geslins often spoke about Mère Gauthier, better known as *"la rabouteuse"* (the faith healer). This mysterious-sounding woman lived alone, not far from our hamlet. Reclusive Mère Gauthier was rumored to be a witch. Despite her reputation, farmers often called upon her to heal sick animals rather than call upon a veterinarian who was not readily available and was expensive. Thus the *rabouteuse* was quite in demand, and was always willing to trade her services for the modest compensation of a goose or a couple of chickens.

I probably would not have met the *rabouteuse*, but for the Geslins' pregnant brown mare who was in labor and unable to deliver. The Geslins, fearing for the life of the animal, sent me running to get hold of the *rabouteuse*. I was relieved to find her at home and told her she was needed at once. After hearing so many tales about Mère Gauthier, I was surprised to see that she was hardly the spooky-looking creature I had imagined I would find. Instead she was a pleasant-looking, soft-spoken woman with gray hair, a round face and clear blue eyes. She promptly grabbed a small black leather case and hurried back to the farm with me.

The Geslins anxiously watched Mère Gauthier as she opened her leather case and carefully laid out small bottles and jars on a bale of hay. She unhurriedly proceeded to stroke the mare's nose, whispering words of encouragement. She then slowly trickled a couple of drops of a brown liquid from one of the vials onto the mare's tongue, while Père Geslin assisted her, firmly holding the horse's mouth wide open.

Everyone anxiously watched the *rabouteuse* rub ointment in a circular motion on the mare's belly while softly chanting incantations. Mère Gauthier repeated the procedure several times, her voice lulling me into trance. The horse was perhaps affected in the same manner, because for the first time she was no longer panting or grunting. Mère Gauthier continued rubbing ointment on the heaving belly until the mare suddenly began to kick her hind legs in the air, her body seized by contractions. The Geslins urged her on in unison and, as though she understood their earnest pleas, the mare powerfully pushed out a gangly colt. It was touching to watch the mother lick her baby, whose long, thin legs were splayed on the ground. Mrs. Gauthier rested on a bale of hay, enjoying the well-earned congratulations of the Geslin family.

I unexpectedly ran into the *rabouteuse* several weeks later. She stopped to greet me, then, noticing that one of my ankles was bleeding, asked how it had happened. I explained it had been a recurrent problem ever since I began wearing clogs. I told her that because my clogs were too large for me, I often scraped the ankle with my other foot, causing a wound that never healed. She looked concerned, took a closer look at my ankle and said she would not let me go without attending to it.

I followed the kind Mrs. Gauthier back to her house. She washed and cleaned my ankle, patted dry the red blister, applied ointment on the wound and wrapped a bandage around it. I thought she was finished with the treatment, but she asked me to stay put. With a mysterious look on her face she fetched a small length of thread, which she looped around my ankle and tied securely with a knot. The *rabouteuse* said that this thread was very special. She solemnly assured me that as long as I wore it I would never scrape my ankle again. I didn't believe in magic, or in talismans, yet Mrs. Gauthier persuaded me there was something special about that thread. I didn't dare remove it, and afterwards her prediction came true. Perhaps not everything can be explained.

10

La Renouardière, July 1943

After Bastille Day it dawned on me that one year had elapsed since the dreaded police roundup and the last time that I was with my mother and father. I missed them terribly and longed to be together with them again. It was as though we had just parted. At times I closed my eyes, making believe that I was with them. I managed to conjure up their presence, clearly seeing my mother and father like I remembered them, reaching for me; then when I could almost feel their touch, my wonderful dream would fade away in a gray, ghostly mist. I tried not to dwell too much on what Mrs. Mounier told me about my parents' arrest, because I hoped for a miracle that would bring me news of their release. I wanted to be strong, to make them proud of me, even if they could no longer see me.

I often thought about how my father, during our long journey across France, remained optimistic, even in the face of adversity, making Alice and me feel that things would get better. I tried to follow his example, doing my best to look at the bright side and not feel sorry for myself.

My optimism was sorely tested, however, when I suddenly developed a painful skin infection. I was fortunate to have remained in good health up to that time, despite the lack of basic hygiene and medical care that prevailed in the country. This infection started rather innocuously, beginning with a rash between my fingers. I thought at first that I had touched the leaves of some *orties*, a poison ivy-like plant growing wild in the fields, which caused a prickly rash that usually vanished overnight. I was not overly concerned until the rash quickly spread over my body and scalp. Soon I was covered from head to toe with red blisters that hardened into ugly scabs. At this point it was obvious that without medical treatment I would never heal. I was burning and feverish.

Mrs. Prim was concerned that my infection could be contagious, and she sent me to the village convent to be examined by Sister Beatrice, who had some medical training. As far as I knew there was no doctor in the village. The nearest one was probably in the nearby county seat of St. Hilaire-du-Harcouet. Sister Beatrice diagnosed my infection as *"la gale"* (scabies). My fever and the infection were too widespread to be treated by her. She gave me a note asking the Mother Superior of the convent of Mortain to admit me to their hospital. I was shocked to learn I was in worse shape than I had imagined. I wondered how I would manage to go to Mortain on foot, as it was at a considerable distance from Savigny-le-Vieux.

Fortunately Mère Geslin came to my rescue and took me to Mortain in her horse-drawn cart. After an interminable ride along rough dirt roads we reached the convent, which was nestled in the countryside. Mère Geslin handed Sister Beatrice's note to the Mother Superior, who, after reading it, assured her I would be looked after at once. I didn't have to wait long in the reception room. A nun came to fetch me. I followed her along vaulted corridors to a room smelling of medication, the first hint that I was in the hospital wing of the convent. As I waited alone in the room I tried to keep calm, but I couldn't stop my growing feeling of apprehension.

Two nuns came marching in, clad in white aprons over black habits. The older nun said that she was Sister Catherine and introduced the younger one as Sister Sophie. Sister Catherine was obviously in charge. She examined me, hovering over me like a huge bird of prey with her flowing habit and the outstretched wings of her hood. She spoke with a gentle voice that belied her stern looks, trying to soothe my fears. "You look like a brave lad. I must tell you that the treatment will hurt, but soon it will be over," she said. With this warning she told me to undress completely, down to my bare buttocks.

The thought of standing naked in front of the two nuns made my head spin, but I had no choice but to comply with her request. Sister Sophie brought a small metal tub into the room and filled it with water. I stepped into the tub totally naked. The nuns rolled up their sleeves and went to work. The procedure was very primitive.

Armed with sponges and cleaning brushes, they began at once to scrub at and wash away the scabs from my body and scalp. The pain was intense, spreading across my body like hot flames, but I bit my lips to hold myself back from screaming. But the humiliation of being seen naked in front of those two nuns was equally painful. Sister Sophie then poured water over my head to rinse away the blood, which streamed down to the bottom of the tub into a crimson pool.

Mercifully, the procedure was finally over. I felt faint, shaking as I stepped out of the tub. After I toweled off, the nuns rubbed my head and body with a strong-smelling mud-like brown paste. I gave them my clothing to be disinfected in exchange for a hospital gown. Still wobbly, I followed Sister Sophie to a dormitory where I was assigned to a bed next to other patients, who were mostly young children. A couple of days after the treatment the burning sensation and soreness were less severe. I was happy to see the redness and blotchiness on my body gradually fade. Sister Catherine continued to give me daily applications of that peculiar brown paste, which did wonders for me.

During the first week I remained in the dormitory. My only distraction was chatting with other patients. My recovery was quick, and by the end of the week the treatment was over and the infection completely gone. All that remained were faint spots on my skin, which I was told would disappear. I was allowed to get dressed. My clothing had been washed, and now smelled clean and fresh. I was restless and asked Sister Catherine's permission to walk outside the dormitory. She granted my request on the condition that I promised to stay out of trouble.

I began surveying the austere-looking convent, tiptoeing along quiet hallways to lessen the noisy clickety-clack of my wooden clogs upon the stone floors. I peeked into a dark chapel where flickering candles revealed the shadowy figures of nuns praying. From this island of silence and solitude I stumbled into a noisy and busy kitchen, where cooks wearing aprons over habits scurried around with steaming pots and platters. Young novices sitting around a long table peeled vegetables while others stamped out what appeared to be cookies from thin sheets of dough; but I realized the cookies were actually holy wafers for parishioners during Mass.

Sister Catherine chatted with me solicitously during my recovery, and when she found out I liked to draw, she brought me a pencil and sheets of paper. I began sketching some of the boys in my dormitory, and soon the word got around that an artist was in their midst. Sister Catherine had probably expected scribbles from me. She was amazed that I had captured the boys' likenesses so well. Before long I had also made drawings of her and other nuns who had heard about my talent.

I had a wonderful time being treated like an instant celebrity. My reputation reached the Mother Superior, who had seen some of the portraits and wanted her own. It was quite an honor to be asked by the head of the convent. Sister Catherine brought me to the sanctuary, where the Mother Superior greeted me warmly, saying that she very much admired the drawing I had done of Sister Catherine. She proceeded to pose for me, holding a prayer book on her lap.

She sat erect, and very still, waiting patiently until I finished. At last I nervously handed her my drawing and waited anxiously for her reaction. I was relieved to see a grin on her lined face. She said that she was quite pleased and, just like Father Perrin, remarked that I was blessed with a wonderful gift from God. She kept me a while longer to chat with me, peering behind thick glasses as she prodded me with questions about my background. I weighed my answers carefully, concerned that she might find out I was Jewish.

It didn't occur to me then the Mother Superior might already have known I was Jewish, especially since Sister Catherine and Sister Sophie had seen me naked and could have reported to her that I was circumcised. I was fortunate they had not let the word out, because many collaborators were eager to denounce Jews to the French police or to the Gestapo.

A couple of weeks later Mère Geslin came to the convent to take me back to Savigny-le-Vieux. Sister Catherine hugged me when I left, saying that she would miss me. I really had come to like her very much, even if she had been the one who worked me over with the scrub brush. After my return from the convent Mrs. Prim was unusually solicitous toward me. Annette and Maurice gave me a hero's welcome and greeted me like their big brother. I was happy to be well again and returned to my daily routine of taking care of chores and spending time with the Geslin family.

11

La Renouardière, November 1943
It was sometime during late fall when I saw American planes flying over Savigny-le-Vieux for the first time. I was with Père Geslin and Roland, working in a field, when the loud roar of engines caught our attention. We looked up, and there etched in the sky were hundreds of glittering bombers, with white stars clearly visible under long wings.

We were awe-struck by the sight of this magnificent armada moving swiftly in tight formation across the sky. We stood motionless for a long time, looking up until the last bombers had vanished out of sight.

This sighting became our main topic of conversation for a while, as well as that of anyone else in the village who had been privileged to witness such an awesome display of American power. Père Geslin was ecstatic. He said that he had no doubt that the American airplanes were headed to Germany on a bombing raid, which raised our hope that the Allies would soon emerge victorious.

In the wake of the American bombers, we saw an inexplicable shower of aluminum strips floating down to the earth. We found those shiny strips just about everywhere, lying on the ground, caught in tree branches and on rooftops. We gathered them in the event that we could find a use for them in the future. Père Geslin, who usually had a ready explanation for everything, was stumped.

Some time later we learned that those mysterious aluminum strips dropped by American airplanes served to scramble the signals of coastal German radar installations. We eventually got used to the sound of American airplanes flying overhead. But if the skies were clear we always ran out to watch the planes gleaming in the sunlight, our hearts filled with good wishes for those brave pilots above. Père

Geslin, who managed to keep us informed about the latest news broadcasts from London, gleefully reported that the Allies were bombing Germany around the clock.

We were jolted from our sleep one night by a thundering noise that shook the house to its very foundation. It sounded like a bomb had fallen nearby. We got up at once, perplexed as to the cause for such a loud noise. The weather outside was calm, and there was no storm in the area that could have accounted for such a powerful jolt.

We stepped outside to check if a tree had perhaps fallen on our roof. It was dark, but we could tell there was nothing amiss with the roof. The same thought must have occurred to the Geslins and to our other neighbors, the Bertrands, who came out with kerosene lanterns, checking farm buildings for possible damage. Everything seemed intact. We were relieved that a meteor had not fallen on us, but we still had no explanation for such a mysterious bang. Perhaps daylight would provide us with some clue about this mystery.

The following morning on his way to work, Père Bertrand stumbled upon the cause of the mysterious jolt. A couple of hundred yards from his farm he had discovered the wreckage of a British bomber in a field. We ran to have a look at the wreckage. The plane's nose had plowed into a hedgerow, and the twisted sections of fuselage and wings were jammed in tree branches, attesting to the force of the impact. The familiar British emblem, a target with red, white and blue circles, was still visible on a crumpled wing panel.

Since there was no trace of bodies, we hoped that the British airmen had been able to parachute to safety before the plane crashed. We speculated that the plane could have been shot by German anti-aircraft fire near the English Channel, or could have gone down because of a mechanical failure.

Later, curious neighbors who had heard about the crash came over to look at the airplane and carry away pieces of the wreckage as souvenirs. The news of the crash must have quickly traveled beyond the village borders, because a couple of days later a German armored car pulled up in front of the Bertrand's farm. From our door we saw Père Bertrand talking and gesturing with soldiers. He told us that he had led them to the crash sight, where they took many photographs of the plane. To our collective relief the German soldiers did not linger around La Renouardière.

We never found out whether the British airmen had survived the crash. There were however, persistent rumors that they were alive, hiding somewhere nearby in the vicinity of Savigny-le-Vieux.

La Renouardière, December 1943

Most of the time Roland Geslin kept to himself and, unlike his father, was not very talkative. But he was good natured, and I enjoyed his company. I felt that he liked me too, and even though I was much younger than he was, he treated me like an equal. Roland was a big help on the farm, and without him his parents would have had to struggle in order to keep up with all the work. Once in a while his father hinted that he was fortunate to have Roland at home, especially since able-bodied young men of his age were compelled to work in German factories. Perhaps the authorities had not caught up with him because he lived in a remote area.

This notion was suddenly dispelled, however, when we learned that a neighbor's son of about Roland's age, who like him had not reported to the authorities, had recently been arrested. Such alarming news rekindled our fear that Roland could be next on the list. The realization that the Germans could strike at will made everybody quite jumpy.

Less than a week later I was outside, drawing water from the well, when I heard the distinctive put-put of a motorcycle. Seconds later, I recognized the unmistakable silhouette of two German soldiers riding a motorcycle with a sidecar. They were coming from the village at the top of our trail. My heart pounding, I dropped my pail at once, and it tumbled to the bottom of the well.

I just had time to run to the Geslins' farm. I found Roland in the barn by sheer luck, up in the loft unloading hay. I screamed at the top of my lungs, "The Boches are coming to get you!" Panic flashed in his eyes. He dropped his fork, jumped to the ground and sprinted outside toward the apple orchard. The sound of the motorcycle grew louder and nearer as I ran from the barn and back to Mrs. Prim's house and hurried through the garden and in through the back door.

I startled Mrs. Prim as I bounded into the house out of breath. I quickly informed her of the situation. At the same time Mrs. Prim heard the approaching motorcycle and through the curtains of the front window saw for herself the two German soldiers. At that moment it occurred to me that I could be in grave danger if the German soldiers had seen me running towards the Geslins' farm and deduced that I was the one who had alerted Roland. I felt a chill run down my spine as I thought that I, too, could be arrested. On an impulse I ran up to the attic and found a hiding place in an old steamer trunk lying among a pile of discarded furniture. I squeezed inside, crouching, keeping the lid cover slightly ajar for air. Under my breath I cursed the mice and rats scurrying across the attic floor. I feared that the creaking floorboards would alert the soldiers if they came into the house to look for me.

I waited without moving for what seemed an eternity until I heard the loud coughing sound of the motorcycle engine. I slithered across the attic floor to one of the small windows and ventured a peek outside. I was relieved to see the two German soldiers heading back to the village without Roland. When I came down from my hideout I found Mrs. Prim shaken by the incident. She said that for a moment she feared retaliation when she saw the German soldiers coming back, their guns at the ready, looking quite agitated and angry.

After this close call, Mère Geslin prepared a little feast to celebrate Roland's escape. Mrs. Prim, the children and I were invited to join the family around a table laden with roast duck and bottles of brandy. Over a generous glass of his best brandy, Père Geslin toasted his son and my quick thinking that had averted his arrest. He recounted to us the harrowing moments when the German soldiers were combing the farm and searching the grounds without success. They were so furious that they had threatened to arrest him or even shoot him if he didn't tell them where Roland was hiding. He was lucky that they didn't carry out their threat, though, because we knew people had been murdered by the Nazis for much less.

La Renouardière, January 1944

My fourteenth birthday came and went unnoticed. I had not told anyone my birthday was on Christmas day, because after arriving in Savigny-le-Vieux I made a conscious effort to divulge as little as possible about myself. While I was not reticent and spoke freely, I was careful to stay away from topics that could lead to my past. I only felt a tinge of sadness, wishing I were with my family to celebrate my birthday. I was fourteen! I realized I was no longer the same young boy who had come to stay with Mrs. Huard. Since then I had learned to cope with the rigors of farm life. The hard work had made me tougher and stronger in the process. My most pressing concern was having grown out of my clothes, which for the most part now looked like rags.

Mère Geslin rescued me once more by giving me some of Roland's old clothes which she had saved from when he was younger. Thus I inherited a pair of pants, a shirt, a corduroy jacket full of patches and a floppy leather cap. These were too large on my smaller frame, however, and I had to secure the billowing trousers around my waist with a length of leather harness I found hanging in the stable. Nonetheless I was thrilled to have inherited such unexpected bounty.

Winter came early, already firmly entrenched in the countryside with icy winds howling across the fields and shivering trees. While I lacked socks and gloves to protect me against the cold, I was able to make do by stuffing rags around my feet inside my clogs and pulling my oversized sleeves down over my fingers.

The days grew short under gloomy gray skies. We routinely got up early and went to bed before nightfall to save the little kerosene we had left to light our lantern in emergencies. I was spending my second winter in the country and grateful for the warmer clothing, which helped me to endure the cold.

La Renouardière, February 1944

I was fortunate that my sister lived within walking distance. Although I could see her only once in a while, knowing that Alice was close by lifted my spirits when I was blue. I managed to take time off to visit her in Alleray for her sixteenth birthday, which fell on February 18.

To celebrate her birthday Mrs. Ledauphin prepared a special lunch with roast duck. I felt privileged to be there with my sister and the Ledauphin family, all of us sitting around the large table and having a good time. Mrs. Ledauphin was as cheerful and loquacious as on the very first day I met her at the bus stop. Even Mr. Ledauphin, who struck me as a quiet man, seemed caught up in the happy mood. I suspected the brandy contributed to his relaxed and jolly frame of mind. Everyone participated in the conversation, even Solange and Wilfrid, who usually took a back seat to their mother. I surprised Alice afterwards by presenting her with a watercolor I had made especially for her birthday, a landscape depicting an apple orchard. The watercolor was passed around the table and drew warm praise from everybody.

Later, when we were alone, Alice and I reminisced about the days at home with our parents and our brother. We managed to dwell only on the good times we had together, remembering some funny incidents and laughing ourselves silly. During those few hours we were once again carefree young people, trying to escape from the dark realities confronting us.

12

La Renouardière, March 1944
Spring was not far away, yet Savigny-le-Vieux was still held tightly in the grip of winter, with slick frozen ground underfoot and a gusty, icy wind blowing in from the English Channel. The only bright spot during those bleak winter days was the occasional get-together with the Geslin family. After the last chores of the day were over, we all gathered around the fireplace in their farmhouse, sitting close to the bright dancing flames, which cast a cheerful glow upon our faces.

Mère Geslin roasted chestnuts in a pan over hot embers while Thérèse served brandy to the adults. Annette and Maurice drank hot cider. Père Geslin insisted that I have a glass of brandy, saying that I deserved to be treated as a grown-up because I worked as hard as one. His compliments and the brandy in my belly ignited a wave of heat rising in my face. My cheeks burned, a small price to pay to be treated like an adult. For a while the only sounds were cracking, peeling and munching of hot chestnuts. Conversations sparked around the circle.

On those occasions Thérèse managed to sit close to me to chat and to be entertained by my banter. I liked her looks and flirted whenever I had a chance to be alone with her. I thought she liked me. I loved the way I made her blush, especially when I saw her cute upturned nose crinkling when she burst out laughing.

La Renouardière, April-May 1944
During early spring there was a resurgence of American bombers crossing the sky high over Savigny-le-Vieux. It was always an event no one wanted to miss. At such times everybody stopped working in order to catch a glimpse of the planes with the beloved white stars under their wings instead of the despised Nazi black swastika. The

bombers passed over us swiftly in orderly "V" formations, like migrating geese headed back home after a long winter. I cheered them in my heart, thinking about those brave American men up in the sky risking their lives for us down below.

In addition to aluminum strips left behind in the wake of the bombers, we also found many leaflets bearing the Cross of Lorraine symbol scattered on the ground. By now just about everyone was familiar with the distinctive design of a cross with two horizontal bars, the rallying symbol for General de Gaulle's Free France movement and the French partisans. It was such an unexpected and exciting find!

Père Geslin solemnly read the leaflet to us, savoring every printed word from his beloved general. It began with an exhortation to all Frenchmen to play their part in helping partisans fight back against the Nazi invaders. Following the general's patriotic call to arms there was uplifting news about the fighting between Allied forces and the Germans, and hopeful predictions that soon the Nazi war machine would be smashed.

However, despite occasional sightings of American bombers overhead and German military convoys driving through the village, it was difficult to think about war or even imagine bombing and destruction. Besides, with the return of spring, the apple orchards ringing la Renouardière were gloriously in full bloom, casting a fragrant spell over the entire countryside.

La Renouardière, June 1944

It was early June when Père Geslin picked up a broadcast from London on his short-wave radio, a brief bulletin announcing that Allied forces had just landed in France and secured a foothold along the Normandy coast. His scraggly face was flushed with excitement when he rounded everybody up to share the startling news. *"Ils ont débarqué!"* (They've landed), Père Geslin cried out, his voice choked with emotion.

We were stunned, overwhelmed by the news of the landing and exhilarated to know we might be liberated soon. In my state of excitement I was already imagining victorious Allied troops marching through Savigny-le-Vieux. In no time it seemed as though everyone else knew about it as well. We were all thirsty to learn more details about the invasion and ready to believe any positive rumors that nourished our hope for a quick Allied victory. The latest rumor was that the fighting was taking place on the coast, about forty miles north of Savigny-le-Vieux. It was always a mystery to me how rumors could spread far and wide in a flash.

The landing was the only topic of conversation, and people took time off from work to share the good news. However, Père Bertrand, our next-door neighbor, who prided himself on being a historian, was only cautiously optimistic and not quite ready to celebrate victory like everybody else. Over generous helpings of Calvados he argued with Père Geslin. Even though he hated *"les Boches"* as much as we did, he was wary of their determination and fighting skills. He pointed out that during World War I the Germans had fought to the bitter end, and recalled that this was not the first time the Allies had attempted to invade France from across the English Channel. I had not been aware that two years before, the Allies had launched a major raid on Dieppe, a harbor town on the northern coast of Normandy, only to be thrown back into the sea by the Nazis.

After the initial news of the landing there was a sudden rash of contradicting rumors making the rounds. Some were of a cheerful nature, while others were downright gloomy. One version had the German troops near collapse, retreating and surrendering. Another version had Allied forces pinned down on the beaches fighting for their survival. It was nerve-wracking to consider the invasion failing. While I remained optimistic and believed with all my heart that the Allies would emerge victorious, I couldn't help but remember Père Bertrand's cautionary comments regarding the German fighting spirit.

Sometime during the middle of June we saw a number of refugees from the Normandy coast who had fled their homes to seek safety in the south, away from the raging battleground. The refugees coming through our area reminded me of the exodus of 1940, with people carrying belongings in every type of conveyance, from horse-drawn wagons to handcarts. Some stopped in the village of Savigny-le-Vieux and at nearby farms, looking for food and temporary shelter. Because we were quite close to the village, some refugees found their way to La Renouardière. The Geslins made room for a family, a couple with four children, while Mrs. Prim volunteered to take in a woman with a small child. These refugees came from St. Mère-Eglise and Carentan, towns located near the coast where the battle was raging.

We were starving for any little bit of news about the course of the invasion. The refugees unfortunately didn't know much more than we did, other than having heard the fierce artillery duels and seen the destruction caused by Allied bombings. They also reported seeing large numbers of German troops and tanks on the road heading to the coast. After the landing took place, we had naively hoped it would be only a matter of weeks until we would be liberated. Much to our dismay, however, we learned from the refugees that in our area of western Normandy the Nazis were not only well entrenched, but also more numerous than we ever imagined.

La Renouardière, June-July 1944

Throughout the month of June we heard only sketchy accounts of the invasion until Père Geslin managed to pick up a news broadcast from London on his short-wave radio. We were relieved to learn that the Allied forces had finally secured a firm foothold on the coast and were pushing back the Germans, although they were still meeting fierce resistance. We had not yet seen any evidence of the invasion, even though some of the fighting was taking place relatively close to us. We suspected that sooner or later the battle would spill over to our area.

It took place in a most dramatic way when, without any warning, the nearby town of St. Hilaire-du-Harcouet was bombed. This picturesque, provincial town about five miles north of Savigny-le-Vieux boasted one of the largest outdoor markets in the region, attended by farmers who came from miles around. I had gone there a couple of times, once with Mrs. Huard when she sold one of her cows and another time with the Geslins.

The day of the bombing I was helping Père Geslin and Roland erect a fence around a pasture. When we heard the drone of airplanes, it seemed like a good excuse to take a break and search the skies for them. We eventually spotted waves of planes in the distance, emerging from a thick cloud cover and flying over the town. Even from afar we recognized American bombers. We were ready to go back to work when we heard powerful explosions rocking the countryside, soon followed by dense spirals of black smoke rising over St. Hilaire-du-Harcouet. It happened so quickly that the three of us were left stunned and speechless. I was reminded at once of another air strike I had witnessed during the exodus, when the town of Châteauneuf-sur-Loire was bombed by the Luftwaffe. How ironic, I thought, for this time around our liberators were the ones raining destruction upon French cities in order to free us from the Nazis.

We really didn't know what to make of the bombing until much later when we heard that St. Hilaire-du-Harcouet was a strategic crossroad and the site of a large concentration of German troops. We had to assume that the air strike was intended to strike the enemy; the bombs were not able to make a distinction between soldiers and civilians. On the way back to the farm, Père Geslin was more upset than I had ever seen him, angrily reacting to what we had just witnessed. He cursed and muttered under his breath: *"Putain de guerre!"* (War is a whore).

A couple of days after the bombing one of the young refugee boys staying with the Geslins became sick. Sister Beatrice, the kind nun I met who had sent me to the convent in Mortain, came over to have a look at the boy. She reassured his parents that with the help of some medication the child would be as good as new.

Unfortunately Sister Beatrice was short of medicine; and because there was no drug store in the village, someone had to go to the nearest one in St. Hilaire-du-Harcouet to fetch it. The parents' worried expression prompted me to volunteer for this errand. I carefully tucked Sister Beatrice's note to the pharmacist into my shirt pocket. On the road to St. Hilaire-du-Harcouet I once more came across the familiar exodus of harried people leaving town.

After the bombing, St. Hilaire-du-Harcouet was an eerie place. The town looked as though a vicious giant had stepped on rooftops and randomly smashed houses. All around the marketplace I noticed that by fate some townhouses bore no visible signs of damage, while others a couple of feet away had collapsed to the ground. Deep craters filled with rubble exuded an acrid odor that permeated the air, making my throat hurt and my eyes tear up. I walked by the remains of burned-out German trucks left as piles of twisted metal. Hardly anyone was left in this desolate setting. I felt like I was stepping into the devil's lair.

I followed Sister Beatrice's excellent directions and easily found the street where the drug store was. Only the corner building with the plaque bearing the street name remained intact. Most of the houses and stores along the street, including the drug store, had been reduced to charred timber, with stones and broken glass littering the cobblestones. There was nothing for me to do but leave this heavy-wrenching scene of destruction as quickly as possible.

On my way back to the village, a German military convoy consisting of trucks and armored vehicles sped by on the narrow country road. In nearly two years in Normandy I'd never seen as many German troops as I encountered on that day. I wondered if those troops were reinforcements heading for the front, or units pulling back.

I was very disappointed that after doing my best to rush to the drug store I had nothing to show for it, except painful blisters on my feet. I wondered what would happen to the young boy without necessary medication. Sister Beatrice fortunately improvised some other way to bring down the child's fever, and soon he was playing with his siblings again. When his parents thanked Sister Beatrice, she insisted it was not her doing, but the Lord's infinite mercy that had restored their boy to good health.

Since the dramatic bombing occurred we were getting used to the stepped-up activity of German military convoys rolling through the village and had become aware of the noise of trucks travelling through la Renouardière. Père Geslin, meanwhile, remained steadfastly optimistic about the outcome of the battle. He chose to believe that the influx of Germans in our area surely meant they were on the run. And yet, despite his unshakable faith in an Allied victory, Père Geslin couldn't dismiss the disturbing fact that two long months had elapsed since the landing, and there was no sign of when we would be liberated.

ABOVE: My mother, Uncle David, one of my mother's sisters, and my father. Poland, 1925.

LEFT TO RIGHT: My father, a co-worker, Uncle David, and other co-workers, assembling watches. Poland, 1924.

ABOVE: *Family portrait of my sister and me with our parents and grandmother Tessie, during her visit from America. Paris, 1935.*
BELOW: *My sister and I, Vincennes, 1934. My mother's identification photo, taken in Montreuil, 1942, before she was deported.*

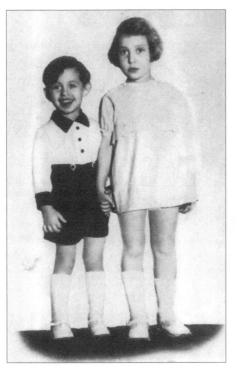

ABOVE: The Eichenbaum's house on rue Villa David in Vincennes, where my parents were married.

RIGHT: The Jewish star I had to wear outdoors and in school.

*The apartment house on rue Colmet-Lepinay in Montreuil,
where we lived until the police roundup of 1942.*

LEFT: *Mrs. Prim's house in Savigny-le-Vieux, near the church.*

BELOW: *Hamlet of La Renouardière. Mrs. Prim's house at the end of the road.*

Some of my wartime sketches from Savigny-le-Vieux, 1943–1944.
ABOVE: *Looking at the road from Mrs. Prim's house.*
Well at right where I fetched water for our daily needs.
BELOW: *Interior view of Mrs. Prim's house at "La Renouardiere."*

"The Virgin with Flowers,"
inspired by icons of the village church.

A sister from Savigny-le-Vieux.

ABOVE: **Mr. Geslin harvesting wheat.**
BELOW: **Bombing during the liberation of Normandy.**

Les Eglantines, the children's home in Jouy-en-Josas.

LEFT *Michel with the Leclère family. St. Aubin-les-Elbeuf, 1943*

BELOW: *Alice, Michel, and I. Jouy-en-Josas, 1948.*

ABOVE: *My elementary school in Vincennes.*
BELOW: *My art school in Paris.*

TOP:
Uncle David,
Aunt Berthe,
Cousin Raoul.
Paris, 1949.

CENTER:
Mr. and Mrs.
Bonneau with their
granddaughter.
Vincennes, 1948.

BOTTOM:
Wedding photo
of Madeleine
Bonneau and
her husband.
Vincennes, 1946.

*Alice, Michel, and I, shortly before leaving for the
United States. Paris, October 1949.*

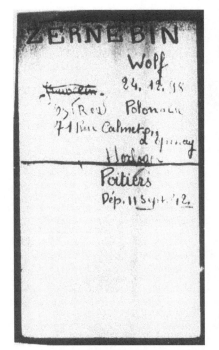
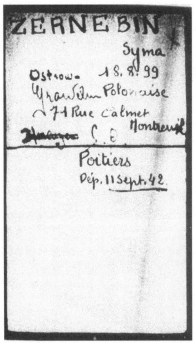

Police record of my parents' arrest in Poitiers while attempting to escape to the non-occupied zone. Our family name has been transcribed incorrectly, yet all other information, such as birthdates, birthplaces, nationality, home address, and even my father's profession of watchmaker, is accurate.

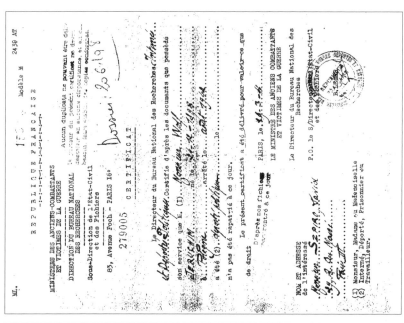

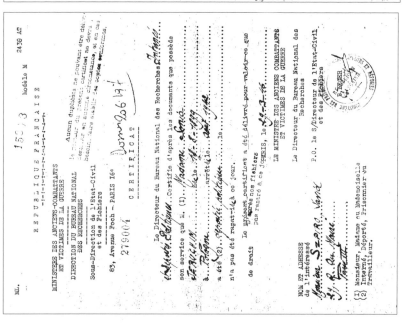

*Affidavits regarding deportation of my mother (left) and father,
dated 1946, issued to my Uncle David, stating that my parents were
arrested and deported in 1942 and had not returned.*

TOP: *Michel and I as new immigrants. New York, 1950.*

TOP RIGHT: *Me, no longer a "greenhorn." Manhattan, 1951.*

BOTTOM: *Cécile and I, just married. Brooklyn, 1956.*

My Army days, from stateside to Korea, 1951–1953.

Liberation

13

La Renouardière, August 1944
I could not wait to visit my sister. I had not seen her since the bombing of St. Hilaire-du-Harcouet, and I missed her terribly. With Mrs. Prim's permission I was on my way to the Ledauphin's farm, a good hour's walk along country roads and byways. About a mile after leaving Savigny-le-Vieux I noticed a German convoy parked along the road ahead. The sight of enemy trucks and German soldiers made me uneasy. I almost turned back, but the desire to see my sister was stronger than my fear. I decided to push forward.

Soldiers in their green battledress were milling about, relaxing, collars open, helmets and rifles scattered on the ground. They were smoking, spread out in the tall grass and enjoying the warm summer day. These men seemed harmless enough, and yet as I walked by them I felt my pulse racing. I made a conscious effort to quiet my growing anxiety, reminding myself that the word "Jew" was not painted on my forehead. Besides, to them I surely looked like any other farmboy with my wooden clogs and tattered clothing.

I pretended to be just a carefree young lad, putting on a happy face for their benefit. I cheerfully waved and yelled out to everyone within earshot *"Bonjour monsieur! Bonjour monsieur!"* as I walked by. The German soldiers looked amused. Some responded with friendly grins, others by tipping their hands in mock salute. I kept up the pretense until the last man was out of sight. I had probably exaggerated the threat facing me, but years in hiding had taught me to be watchful and on guard.

I only began to relax when I was far away at the end of the road. I was still thinking about my encounter when the roar of engines shattered the silence around me. Five fighter planes suddenly materialized out of a cloud bank. Coming in my direction, they quickly

141

loomed larger, then screamed overhead and flew toward the German convoy.

It was the closest look at American planes I had ever had. The white stars and other markings were clearly visible under the wings. These aircraft, however, were so unusual-looking with their twin fuselages that I wondered if I had imagined them. Such a futuristic design could have been inspired by a Jules Verne novel! As quickly as they arrived, the fighter planes vanished over the horizon. They were gone for a while, and then I once more heard the growling sound of engines. I scanned the skies until I spotted them flying together in tight formation, coming back my way along the same flight path.

The attack came swiftly. Without any warning each fighter plane took its turn, peeling back from the formation and swooping down toward the earth, machine guns blazing away. Suddenly it came to me—the German convoy I could no longer see from my vantage point must have been their target!

All at once thundering explosions jolted the quiet day, followed by red-orange flames and black smoke rising above the area. Seconds later the fighter planes regrouped and roared away, apparently having completed their mission.

As I watched dark smoke billowing in the sky, I thought about those German soldiers I'd just seen resting by the roadside and wondered how many were now wounded or dead. It seemed that blind fate had once more kept me out of harm's way while allowing death to visit those German soldiers. At that moment I should have been celebrating their demise because they were the despised enemy, yet I felt strangely subdued, remembering their young, friendly faces and greetings.

The Ledauphins welcomed me like a member of their family as usual. I was very happy to be with my sister and share my latest adventures with her. We both hoped that we would be liberated soon. We indulged ourselves in talking about the day when we would be back home with our parents and Michel, despite the fact that we had no further news about the fate of our parents since Mrs. Mounier told us they were arrested.

In Savigny-le-Vieux, the strafing of the German convoy took center stage for the next couple of days. We heard there had been many casualties and much destruction of material. Père Geslin was fascinated by my description of the American fighter planes with the strange twin fuselages. That story, however, was soon eclipsed by the Allied capture of the strategic towns of St. Lo and Coutances to the north. But more significantly, we heard that Allied forces were within striking distance of the town of Avranches, a mere fifteen miles from us. As the battle came closer to Savigny-le-Vieux, we began hearing the thundering of artillery barrages for the first time.

On the morning of August 6, the possibility of American soldiers marching into la Renouardière never entered my mind. I was going about my chores in a pasture near the Geslin's farm, gathering tender shoots for our hungry rabbits. I hardly noticed the barnyard sounds and the faraway rumbling of artillery guns, when voices close to me instantly got my attention.

I climbed onto the nearest hedgerow and was surprised to find myself almost face to face with a squad of helmeted soldiers walking slowly through the field, guns at the ready. The sudden realization that they were American soldiers sent a wave of emotion coursing through my body. I felt tears of happiness well up in my eyes. I was still stunned by this extraordinary encounter when a soldier signaled me to come over. I found myself surrounded by tall men in light khaki uniforms, grimy and unshaven, but to my eyes as handsome as Greek gods.

One soldier began asking me questions but soon realized I didn't understand a word of English. Another soldier took over the questioning by demonstrating what they wanted: removing his canteen from his belt, he turned it upside down to show me it was empty. To show him I understood what he meant, I mimicked drinking from a glass. My little pantomime elicited general laughter punctuated with a loud chorus of *"Oui, oui, oui!"*

I pointed in the direction of the farm, motioning the G.I.s to follow me. It was one of the proudest moments of my life when the Geslins witnessed my grand entrance in their courtyard with the Americans in tow. Their bewildered expressions quickly turned to happy faces as they rushed over to greet the soldiers, anxious to quench their thirst. I was about to lead them to the well, but Mère

Geslin insisted such special guests deserved better than drinking plain water. *"Entrez, entrez messieurs!"* (Come in, come in gentlemen). She waved them into the farmhouse, her face flushed with excitement.

I at once alerted Mrs. Prim, Annette and Maurice, and also our neighbors to the arrival of the Americans. Everyone reacted incredulously at first until I persuaded them that it was real. Excited and joyful, everyone rushed to the Geslin's farm. It was quite a sight! The entire community of la Renouardière was assembled in the farmhouse, gawking at the brave soldiers who had come all the way from America to free us from the Nazis.

Mère Geslin and Thérèse attentively refilled glasses, blushing as soldiers thanked her with grateful smiles. Not to be left out of the limelight, Père Geslin toasted *"A nos amis Americains!"* (To our American friends!) and proceeded to shake hands with each soldier. Emboldened by his example everyone eagerly joined in, the women following the local custom of kissing them twice on both cheeks. To thank us the G.I.s took chocolate bars and chewing gum from their packs and passed them around, along with cigarettes for the men.

For the next couple of days we were still talking about the "Ricains," as we affectionately nicknamed the G.I.s. We hoped that it would be just a matter of time until the main forces followed. About a week later our wishes were granted, as American convoys began pouring through Savigny-le-Vieux.

Their arrival was officially greeted by a carillon of church bells. At last we were liberated! The Geslins, the Bertrands, Mrs. Prim, the children and I rushed to the village to take part in the celebration. We joined a crowd of villagers and farmers lining the road, cheering wildly as the G.I.s slowly rode by in dust-covered jeeps and trucks. Young women threw kisses and flowers at the smiling G.I.s, who reciprocated by waving back and handing out chocolate and chewing gum as they rode by.

After we were liberated it was rumored that a band of German soldiers had been seen wandering around Savigny-le-Vieux. Père Geslin speculated that they were either deserters or stragglers cut off from their units. It was alarming to think they could be in our own backyard, armed and possibly dangerous.

Days later I couldn't believe my own eyes when, in plain view, three German soldiers hurriedly walked through the orchard by the Bertrand's farm and disappeared. I alerted Mrs. Prim and our neighbors at once. Everyone was shocked and concerned, but helpless to prevent German soldiers from roaming the countryside.

The news of my sighting must have traveled beyond our hamlet, because shortly after this incident two men on bikes came knocking at our door. Wearing caps and old corduroy jackets, they looked like typical farmers except for the guns strapped on their backs and their armbands with the Cross of Lorraine emblem. They were two of the famous French partisans we'd heard so much about.

The tallest man, who wore a mustache, said that he was Eugene Brossac and his companion was Marcel, his brother. They came from the nearby village of Breil. They had heard of the recent sighting of German soldiers in the area, and they were trying to track them down. Having heard that the Germans had been seen around la Renouardière, they had come down at once, hoping to get a fresh lead that could help them find the stragglers.

Mrs. Prim urged me on. "Tell those *brave messieurs* what you saw!"

"I only had a glimpse—no, I couldn't tell if the soldiers had guns, nor where they went," I replied, sorry to be unable to help. Eugene stroked his mustache as though he was pondering my explanation. "The Germans still could be around. We have to make sure!" He then looked me straight in the eye. "You look like a smart lad—you must know the area like the back of your hand," insisting I had to help them find the soldiers. "It's everyone's patriotic duty!" Marcel chimed in. How could I possibly refuse to help without sounding unpatriotic or like a coward?

In my mind there was only a slim chance that we would ever find the German soldiers. I kept that thought to myself, careful not to irritate Eugene, who managed to intimidate me with his brusque manner.

I pondered where to go next. Strictly on a hunch, I guided the partisans along a footpath to the top of a ridge overlooking a brook several hundred yards below. It was a good vantage point from which to see the entire countryside. I often took this path to the brook to wash our clothes and bathe. We paused to look around. There was no sign of life other than a herd of cows resting under shady trees in the distance.

We were about to backtrack when Marcel pulled his brother by the sleeve and whispered, *"On a trouvé les Boches!"* (We've found the Krauts!). He pointed toward the brook below. I shielded my eyes from the sun and saw clothing scattered on the ground. The clothing was hardly noticeable because it blended almost perfectly with the grass: dark green, just like German uniforms! The soldiers must have been bathing because suddenly they emerged from the brook, bare-chested, wearing only underwear.

Not wasting any time, Eugene unstrapped his rifle, took aim and fired several rounds in their direction. I was probably as startled and scared by the noise as the German soldiers were. They immediately raised their arms, waving frantically in a sign of surrender. Eugene and his brother sprinted down the slope with their guns pointed at the Germans. I felt I had done my patriotic duty and hurried back to La Renouardière, afraid to witness bloodshed.

A while later the two brothers came back to retrieve their bikes, preceded by the three German soldiers holding their hands clasped over their heads. Without helmets they looked more like harmless teenagers than dangerous warriors. Everyone in La Renouardière came out to watch the partisans parading their prisoners. We heard later that the German soldiers were turned over to the Americans, and their lives were spared.

14

La Renouardière, August-September 1944

Day after day American convoys passed through Savigny-le-Vieux, speeding toward unknown destinations. It was no longer a novelty to hear the continuous drone of trucks coming from the village. However, there was renewed excitement when we heard that an infantry unit had stopped in the area and set up camp in a nearby pasture. Villagers flocked there to greet them. Unfortunately the camp was off limits, with rolls of barbed wire stretched around to keep curious onlookers like us at bay. After the infantry unit was gone, Père Geslin suggested we look at the abandoned campsite to see if some discarded pieces of equipment had been left behind.

Père Geslin hitched his horse and wagon, and he, Roland and I rode together to the field. We found dozens of large khaki drums, empty cartridge metal boxes and crushed tin cans half-buried in a ditch. Père Geslin thought the drums could be useful. It took the three of us to lift the heavy drums onto the wagon. We were just about to leave when I discovered a pup tent that had escaped our initial inspection flattened on the ground.

Père Geslin generously said that since I found the tent it was only fair that it should be mine. I scrubbed the mud and grime off the canvas until it looked brand new. I was wondering what to do with such a valuable find when a wonderful idea came to me, inspired by the American army uniform I so admired. If only I could find a seamstress willing to make a jacket and a pair of pants out of this piece of canvas, I could look like my heroes!

It occurred to me that Mrs. Plantin, who lived in the village, was a good friend of Mrs. Prim and also a fine seamstress. Filled with trepidation, I went to the village to see Mrs. Plantin with my precious khaki bundle. I told her I lived with Mrs. Prim and hoped she would be willing to make me a suit. She was amused at my excited state when I described to her what I had in mind. She laid out the canvas on a table, examined it through her thick glasses and squeezed the material between her fingers. She chuckled "It will be a miracle if I can even sew such stiff material." She took my measurements, which she carefully entered in a notebook.

I was already visualizing myself in a stylish jacket and pants like the G.I.s', but before entertaining such a dream, I needed to deal with the thorny question of payment. I told Mrs. Plantin that I had no money, but in exchange I would do any task that she required. I anxiously waited for her answer. Much to my surprise she said that she knew Mr. and Mrs. Crochet quite well and had admired my watercolors in their house. She loved flowers and was willing to trade her services for a watercolor of a vase with roses.

I eagerly accepted her offer. I couldn't have been happier when after several fittings, the much-anticipated day arrived. The fit was perfect. Although the stiff canvas material hindered my movements, this was a small price to pay for such a handsome outfit. I kept admiring myself in the mirror: a slender boy with thick dark hair, grinning from ear to ear, smartly dressed in a tailored waist-high khaki jacket and long pants with extra large pockets like I'd seen on American uniforms.

Without access to newspaper or radio, we still relied on rumors to follow the invasion's progress. Through the grapevine we kept ourselves somewhat informed of the latest developments. We heard more good news about Allied victories toward the end of August, beginning with the capture of the strategic towns of Argentan and Le Mans and culminating with the liberation of Paris. I was thrilled by such wonderful news, imagining the people there dancing in the streets. Père Geslin felt that it was the turning point of the invasion and that soon the Nazis would lay down their arms.

During those dramatic times my life at La Renouardière was still very much the same. However, the liberation of Paris reawakened my longing to go home, a feeling that I had managed to suppress since coming to Savigny-le-Vieux. Nonetheless, I was realistic enough to know that there were many obstacles ahead before my wishes could become reality.

Since the Nazis were no longer in Paris I felt that I would not be compromising my security or that of my sisters by writing to the Bonneaus for permission to leave Savigny-le-Vieux. I was hoping that they would let me stay with them until my parents were liberated by the Allies. I believed that they were still alive somewhere in a labor camp in Germany.

In the middle of September the village mailman made a surprise visit to La Renouardière. It was such a rare occurrence for anyone to get mail. There was a letter for me! I could hardly contain my excitement as I read Mrs. Bonneau's reply, while Mrs. Prim, dying of curiosity, peered at me from behind her glasses. Mrs. Bonneau wrote that she and her husband were looking forward to having me back; however, my return would have to wait until travel was normalized. She explained that most transportation was disrupted because of the liberation. She urged me to be patient and promised that I would soon be able to go back and see my brother again. I was in high spirits, while Mrs. Prim looked glum after hearing the gist of my letter.

I looked forward to visiting my sister and showing her the letter. On my way to Alleray I was still mulling over Mrs. Bonneau's comments regarding the lack of transportation. The prospect of having to wait weeks, perhaps months, until trains were running again left me in a funk. All of a sudden an idea came to me: What if I could borrow my sister's bike to go to Vincennes?

As I expected, Alice thought that I was foolish and my plan far fetched. "Without a sou in your pocket, how do you expect to pay for food and shelter along the way?" she argued. I should have listened to her sound advice, but my desire to return to Paris made me overlook common sense. I spent the next hours cajoling and begging her to reconsider. I couldn't tell for sure what made her change her mind, but I suspected that my earnestness, enthusiasm and above all my confidence in being able to make it back finally won her over.

We hugged each other. I held back my tears, trying to show Alice that I was quite determined and ready to tackle the journey. I promised to write as soon as I reached Vincennes. The Ledauphins wished me good luck. On my way back to the village I savored the pleasure of riding a bike again. I was elated as miles quickly vanished behind me. Mrs. Prim was crestfallen when she heard my plan, but she couldn't keep me from leaving. I spent the last couple of days in Savigny-le-Vieux saying goodbye to people who had shown me compassion. I went to see Mr. Crochet and returned the books he had loaned me. I was pleased to notice my watercolors displayed in his classroom. The Geslins were saddened that I was leaving, and Annette and Maurice looked forlorn.

I asked Père Geslin if he could help me plan an itinerary, but he confessed that he had never ventured beyond the county. He suggested asking the café owner, "A man who traveled far and wide in his youth," he added. Père Mercier was most obliging. Between serving customers, he wrote down the names of towns on the way to Paris and gave it to me as a travel guide.

It was time for me to pack my few items of clothing. I made them into a roll into which I carefully placed my watercolor set, sketch pad and drawings. I tied the small bundle behind the bike seat. The Geslins gave me a loaf of bread, some paté, and filled my goat-skin flask with cider. I thought the food ought to last a while— after that I would have to improvise and trust my good fortune for the rest of the trip.

Père Geslin's voice choked as he toasted to my safe return. *"Gars Simon, tu va nous manquer!"* (Lad Simon, we'll miss you). Mère Geslin, Thérèse and Roland nodded earnestly with the same sentiment. Looking in their eyes I knew I was going to miss those plain farmers who had helped me forget my loneliness through their friendship. I then turned to Mrs. Prim, who deserved some special recognition. I thanked her for having looked after me. Annette and Maurice stood by looking forlorn, tears rolling down their cheeks. After more hugs and handshakes it was time for me to go.

I didn't think that I would feel sad leaving, yet I felt a twinge in my chest. Halfway up the hill I turned around for a last look at La Renouardière. It dawned on me that it had been just about two years since I set foot in Savigny-le-Vieux.

I rode by the tiny house near the old weathered church. Soon I had left Savigny-le-Vieux and was headed for the road going to the nearby village of Buais. From there Père Mercier had assured me that I would easily find *la grande route* (the main highway).

After reaching Buais I found the entrance of the highway blocked by jeeps and American military police, who waved me away. At a village café someone suggested an alternate route to reach Domfront, the next town on my itinerary. He said the most direct way to Paris was the highway used by American convoys; unfortunately as I had discovered earlier, it had been declared off limits to civilians.

Because of this unexpected detour I covered twice as much distance along small dirt trails to reach Domfront. During my trip I experienced many similar frustrating detours and occasionally got lost along the byways. It took me well over a week to reach the town of Verneuil, which, according to Père Mercier, was the midpoint of my trip.

By then my bread and paté were long gone. I relied on the good will of farmers who were willing to trade food for work. I was willing to do any menial chores. I cleaned stables, loaded hay, and stacked wood. On rare occasions I couldn't find an accommodating farmer and went to sleep on the roadside with an empty stomach.

To quench my thirst I stopped at public pumps in villages along the way or looked for farms, where I was sure to find cool water. Late in the afternoon I began searching for a place to spend the night. Farmers usually allowed me to sleep in a barn or stable. At the end of each day I was so leg-weary that I could have slept anywhere and felt lucky just to have a roof over my head, even when I had to share my bed of hay with insects who, resenting my intrusion, attacked me mercilessly.

Without a map I had to trust any stranger willing to direct me to the next town. Most people I encountered were helpful and pointed me in the right direction. However there were others, well-intentioned but misinformed, who sent me in the opposite direction, adding long and tiring miles to my journey.

By the second week of my trip I considered myself fortunate to have traveled miles and miles over bumpy and treacherous dirt and gravel roads without experiencing any mechanical problems. Alice's bicycle held up beyond my wildest expectations until I found myself stranded in the middle of nowhere with my first flat tire.

There was not a soul in sight, only fields reaching out to the horizon. Hours later I found a village. Once more luck smiled upon me. The only bike shop in the village was open and had a generous owner who came to my rescue. Even though I told him I had no money, he repaired my flat and gave me a handful of *rustines* (small rubber patches) to take along, just in case I got stuck again.

I rode through many towns and villages that bore the terrible scars of the invasion. Houses reduced to rubble and burnt timber were mute witnesses to the savage fighting that had swept through Normandy. I had not seen such heartbreaking devastation since the bombing of St. Hilaire-du-Harcout. I dared not think about the poor people who had died trapped in the firestorm.

By the end of the second week my pulse quickened as I neared Paris. There were signs indicating that the towns I was passing were ones from when we went on vacation to Richebourg. There were more houses lining the road and also more traffic, with buses and cars moving at a fast pace and spewing black diesel fumes as they drove by. I hugged the roadside to keep out of their way. However, the most commonly used transport was bikes. One afternoon I was passing the roadside factories as a shift ended, and was caught up in a horde of bikers heading home.

A youngish-looking man riding next to me gave me a friendly hello and inquired if I was a farmboy, pointing to the wooden clogs I was wearing and obviously curious about my general appearance. Under his prodding I succinctly told him where I had come from and where I was headed. By chance he was well acquainted with western Normandy, and he was amazed that I had ridden so far. According to his calculations I must have traveled well over two hundred miles. When he found out I had nowhere to sleep, he invited me to spend the night in his house.

I have forgotten his name, but not his hospitality. This affable stranger lived with his wife and young son in a modest cottage. His wife served us a delicious dinner, my first good meal in weeks. Because I had survived mostly on bread and water, I ate too fast and too much at once, and my stomach suddenly cramped under the sudden onslaught of food. Thankfully the pain didn't last.

I was also able to wash at a sink with running water and use a fragrant bar of soap to scrub away layers of dust and grime. It was incredibly luxurious! I slept blissfully that night on a comfortable mattress in the attic. The next morning my generous hosts treated me to a breakfast like I used to have at home, a steaming bowl of café au lait and a freshly baked baguette.

I bid my good Samaritans goodbye and left the suburbs of Argenteuil for the last leg of my journey. The thought of finally reaching the end gave a new spring to my legs and sent my spirits soaring. As I came closer to Paris the road became even more congested, crowded with cars, buses and military vehicles speeding by dangerously close.

At last the city skyline appeared in the distance. I was so excited that my heart raced wildly when I spotted the Eiffel Tower looming high over the horizon.

Finding my way across Paris turned out to be more of a challenge than I had imagined, especially with the maze of streets going every which way, pulsating with crowds and maddening traffic. I ran into barricades blocking streets and got lost in confusing detours. Military traffic signs in English were posted everywhere, reminding me that not long ago the sign had been in German, with the dreaded swastika symbol.

With the help of passersby I somehow managed to head in the right direction. Once I reached the Place de la Republique I was confident that I could find my way to Vincennes. I rode past Nation, Cours de Vincennes, and to the old medieval château. I suddenly became exhilarated, feeling the realization of my dream within my grasp. Yet I was apprehensive at what the Bonneaus' reception might be, as they had not been alerted to my sudden return.

The stately chestnut trees lining the boulevard and the nearby park brought back happy memories of my father, Alice and me riding together along meandering bicycle paths. I rode by the ornate Vincennes city hall, then followed quiet narrow streets to the old neighborhood where I had lived as a young boy. Before realizing it I had turned the corner and arrived at the Bonneaus' house. Time had slightly blurred the image that I had of their house, but I vividly remembered the window to the right of the entrance, and the last vision of my parents and their friends waving goodbye from behind the parted curtains.

I quickly dried the tears running down my cheeks, leaned my bike against the house and stepped up to the front door. I rang the doorbell, holding my breath with anticipation. I had a feeling of déjà vu when the door slowly opened and Mrs. Bonneau appeared, restraining her two dogs, who were growling and barking at me. She was smaller and grayer than I had remembered. She looked me over, cautiously, questioningly. Had I changed so much, I wondered? But after all, two years was a long time, and back then I had still been a young boy.

I shouted my name in order to be heard over the din of the dogs. Mrs. Bonneau's guarded expression changed to a wide grin, her pale gray eyes brightening as she finally recognized me. She hugged me, her slender body pressing against mine.

She turned around and excitedly called out into the hallway: *"Papa, Madeleine, venez vite, nôtre petit Simon est de retour!"* (Father, Madeleine, come quick, our little Simon is back!).

The Bonneaus

15

Vincennes, October 1944
At first the Bonneaus looked startled, obviously at a loss to compre-hend how I'd managed to get back to Vincennes on my own. After the initial shock subsided, Mrs. Bonneau and Madeleine were all smiles. They hugged me like a lost son, while Mr. Bonneau, who was more reserved, greeted me with a warm handshake.

I was relieved that the Bonneaus did not reprimand me for tak-ing matters into my own hands, a nagging fear that had weighed on my mind since leaving Savigny-le-Vieux. I was aware that they would have been entirely justified to be mad at me for ignoring their instructions. I had not forgotten their letter in which they had writ-ten that as soon as train travel resumed, they would send Mrs. Mou-nier to Savigny-le-Vieux to take Alice and me back to Vincennes. I should have felt some guilt over my transgression, but at that mo-ment I was too excited that my bike trip finally was over to let those thoughts intrude upon the celebration.

After dinner the Bonneaus pressed me with questions, wanting to know how I had managed to find food and shelter during my journey, and wondering if I had ever been in danger. They listened attentively to my story as I recounted how I had trusted fate and generally found compassionate farmers along the way who were will-ing to help me. I also described some of the places I'd seen along the way. The Bonneaus had been spared from the ravages of bombs and artillery fire, and my description of battle-scarred villages and towns in Normandy filled them with melancholy. Across the dining room table Mr. and Mrs. Bonneau looked at me pensively while Madeleine wiped away some tears.

When I finished telling my story a pall of sadness lingered, everyone lost in his or her own silent thoughts. Finally Mr. Bonneau

157

broke the spell and urged his wife and daughter to cheer up and officially welcome my return. Lifting his wine glass he made a toast, solemnly declaring *"Au petit Simon."* He then made a little speech in which he congratulated me on my enterprise and tenacity. It took me by surprise. All at once I felt myself blushing and my ears burning. It had been a long time since anyone had complimented me.

I felt a gentle drumming of fingers on my back, and Madeleine's voice pulled me out of my sleep. I woke with a start. Although my nightmare was already fading away, some terrifying images were still clinging in my mind, visions of myself helplessly trapped in Mrs. Prim's house as a bomb exploded, ripping the roof and walls apart. I looked up. Madeleine was hovering over me, tousling my hair and pulling off my blanket. She laughingly admonished me, "Hurry up, sleepyhead, or you'll be late for school!"

I quickly got dressed in some of the hand-me-down clothing that Mrs. Bonneau had gotten from her church. These garments had replaced my old ones, which were ill-fitting and becoming threadbare. But best of all were my newly acquired shoes and socks. I had dreamt for a long time of the day when I would finally be able to discard my wooden shoes for a pair of regular shoes. Wearing them was heavenly!

I ran downstairs and quickly washed at the bathroom sink, enjoying the luxury of hot running water and the feel and smell of the freshly laundered towel against my face. In the kitchen Mrs. Bonneau was already pouring coffee in a bowl for me. *"Bonjour Tante,* I am sorry I'm late," I said, looking as contrite as possible. She smiled because I had remembered to address her as Aunt. To Mrs. Bonneau it was important that I thought of myself as a member of their family instead of calling them *monsieur* and *madame.* From then on it was *Tante* and *Oncle.*

Because of the timing of my arrival Mrs. Bonneau was able to get me enrolled in my grade level just in time at the local *école secondaire.* She persuaded the principal that I would be able to catch up even though I had missed two years of schooling. And so, within a week after I arrived in Vincennes, I was once again a student.

At times I had to pinch myself to make sure I was not dreaming.

Savigny-le-Vieux seemed so distant, and yet barely a month before I had been attending to my daily chores, trudging along in my wooden shoes and carrying pails of water and stacks of wood. Practically overnight I had been given the chance to lead the normal life of a schoolboy.

Yet despite my best efforts to integrate into my new life, the transition was painfully slow. I didn't mingle easily with the other boys. At times I felt like an intruder. Perhaps I was still afraid that my Jewish identify would be revealed, even though I knew that I had nothing to fear anymore. Deep down, I wished very much to be like one of them, going about life seemingly without a care in the world. But for me it was a slow process to try to extricate myself from the person I had become, watchful and wary of strangers.

I had missed two years of schooling, and catching up with my studies was an uphill climb, especially in science and math, subjects that I had never tackled before. Math had been my Achilles' heel in the past, and time had not improved my aptitude for it. Fortunately for me, Mr. Bonneau took a great interest in my schoolwork—especially algebra, because of his engineering background.

I often reflected about the overnight changes in my life, the comforts and the warmth of a family who genuinely cared about me. But as wonderful as those changes were, it still took some adjustment to cope with the Bonneaus' way of life. In contrast to the way I had lived in Savigny, where I had been treated as a servant but otherwise left on my own, it was difficult to suddenly be the focus of attention and to have to live by strict rules.

Dining was formal. The main meal was lunch. I came back from school at the same time that Mr. Bonneau and Madeleine came home from work. I had to relearn proper table manners. In Savigny-le-Vieux I had picked up the food with my knife and wiped my mouth on my sleeve. Now I had to make sure to select the proper utensil and wipe my mouth with a napkin. "No slurping! Elbows off the table!" commanded Mrs. Bonneau. She never missed a thing.

Meanwhile, as usual, Mr. Bonneau monopolized the conversation as he rambled on about the war, politics and the threat of communism. I had no idea what communism was all about, but according to him the communists were as big a threat as the Nazis.

Mrs. Bonneau was all business, efficiently serving and keeping an eye on the kitchen for the next course to come. Madeleine would interrupt her father with lighthearted conversation about her work. Mr. Bonneau found it difficult to stop her chatter when she got started. I was glad Madeleine was there, always bringing sunshine and mirth to the table. She had a cheerful personality, not like her parents, who were serious and not much given to laughter. Madeleine would smile and wink at me, aware that I enjoyed and appreciated her humorous banter.

The Bonneaus' house was comfortable and tastefully furnished. Polished wooden floors and thick Oriental rugs lent a welcoming look to the cozy, bourgeois interior. The pervasive smell of floor reminded me of our apartment in Montreuil and how my mother had taken pride in her impeccably polished floors.

The front parlor was a constant reminder of my parents and the fateful day in July 1942 when we met the Bonneaus for the first time. Now the room was empty and quiet, but somehow I still felt their lingering presence. I wistfully hoped that the room would suddenly become alive again and that they would be there with me. It was only a silly fantasy. I knew I could not turn back the clock. The topic of my parents was not easily broached by the Bonneaus or myself. There was little they could have said. Without fresh news concerning their fate, speculation was painful and, in the end, useless.

As soon as I could I wrote to my sister and brother to inform them that I had safely arrived in Vincennes. I tried to be patient because I knew that the mail was still terribly slow and unreliable. I kept my fingers crossed, hoping that my letters would get to them soon. Since I arrived it seemed that every day brought something new into my life. For instance, the Bonneaus had decided I should be more involved with other boys, and so they made me join a troop of Protestant Boy Scouts affiliated with their church.

I was proud to wear the Boy Scout uniform given to me by the church, pleased by the colorful scarf and badges sewn onto my shirt sleeves. Although I was readily accepted as a new member by the scoutmaster and the troop, I still felt like an outsider, especially when we prayed before meetings or sang Christian hymns. I felt the same way on Sundays when we went to church. I was somewhat uncomfortable, for I knew I didn't belong there. But I didn't think the Bonneaus were trying to indoctrinate me into the Protestant religion; they merely wanted to include me in family activities.

As I sat in one of the pews during a service it struck me that, in contrast to the elaborate pageantry of the Catholic Mass I had experienced in Savigny-le-Vieux, the service in this Huguenot church exuded simplicity. The pastor wore a black suit, unlike the fancy vestment worn by the priest. And instead of reciting prayers in Latin and delivering sermons full of complicated biblical references, the pastor spoke plainly to the congregation.

16

Vincennes, November 1944

One day, when I came back from school, Mrs. Bonneau told me with a deadpan expression that I had forgotten something on the kitchen table. She didn't offer any clue. I rushed in and found letters from my sister and my brother. My heart pounded with joy. I was so happy! My hand trembled as I opened the envelopes. Mrs. Bonneau smilingly tried to calm me down.

Alice had written several letters; she was well and her life was pretty much the same. Nothing exciting to tell, she said, unlike my adventures. She missed me a lot and couldn't wait to leave the farm. Did I have any news about when Mrs. Mounier would be able to get her? She was envious that I went to school and hoped that soon she too would resume her studies. She said she had told Mrs. Prim and the Geslins that I had made it safely to Vincennes.

The other letter was from Michel. It was the first time I had heard from him since the summer of 1942. When I left him he was only five. Two years in the life of a child is a long time.

I hardly could believe it was my little brother who had written such a well-composed letter, with fine penmanship and few spelling mistakes. I was impressed by his maturity. Michel wrote that he was excited to hear from me and couldn't wait to see me. As I had explained to him in my last letter, he understood that Alice was still in Normandy and that our parents were in a labor camp, unable to contact us. But I reassured him that as soon as the war was over our family would be together again. I was glad he took my optimistic explanations in stride.

In his letter Michel listed all of his activities—school, soccer and after school play. He said that he liked school very much and was at the top of his class. As an incentive, Mrs. Leclère rewarded him with five francs to put away in his piggy bank every time he had a good report card. The piggy bank was almost full, he said, and perhaps he would soon have enough money to buy himself a pair of roller skates. I broke out in laughter when he suggested that, like Mrs. Leclère, I reward him for his good grades.

He also mentioned that he was doing fine, had enough to eat every day, and had grown quite a bit since I saw him last time. As a matter of fact, Mrs. Leclère had just bought him a new coat and another pair of shoes. Mr. and Mrs. Leclère almost never yelled at him, except when he got into some mischief (not too often, he wrote). He liked Gaston a lot because he was very nice and spent time with him after work.

My brother's letter lifted my spirits, because I sensed that despite our separation he seemed well-adjusted and reasonably happy with the Leclère family. What luck that such decent people had come his way! I asked Mr. Bonneau if he could arrange for me to visit my brother. He reminded me that obtaining a train pass was nearly impossible then. I had anticipated his answer, but I was so anxious to see Michel that I was hoping he could have worked a miracle. "I understand how you feel, *mon petit Simon*—but you need patience. Trust me, my wife and I are doing the best we can for you."

Vincennes had almost returned to normal. Although rationing was still in effect and people had to wait in long lines outside neighborhood stores, it was a small price to pay for freedom. We seldom saw American soldiers in our neighborhood, but we were told that troops were lodged in the medieval château near the metro. I made a mental note to walk over there after school to see for myself (with the Bonneaus' permission, of course) and ask Fernand, my new friend, to come along.

I'd met Fernand in church after the Sunday service a few weeks before. The Bonneaus had decided to remain for a while, having refreshments and chatting with other parishioners in the adjoining meeting hall.

Fernand and I hit it off right away when we found out we went to the same school and belonged to the same Boy Scout troop, which I had just joined. He was a year older than I, gangly, and behind his glasses he had a perpetual twinkle in his eyes. I liked his easygoing way.

We met at his home or at the Bonneaus'. One of our favorite activities was to practice Morse code together, hoping to be good enough one day to be awarded merit badges. In a darkened room we took turns using a flashlight to send messages. We used a technique that we had been taught, covering the lens of the flashlight with the palm of one hand and releasing it slowly or quickly, thus spelling out words. The recipient had to jot down on a pad what he thought was transmitted. Often enough Fernand and I were confused about the duration of the flash of light, which in turn changed the intended message. Fortunately we didn't take our mistakes too seriously, but usually had a good laugh over our confusion.

Another pastime we enjoyed was practicing tying knots, following the diagrams in the Boy Scout manual. Then, when we had gained enough confidence in our skills, we attempted each complicated twisting and looping without the guide.

Back in Savigny-le-Vieux I had been cut off from the outside world for such a long time that I had not been aware the war had spread all around the world. I was startled to learn that America had been fighting on so many fronts, not just in Europe, but also in the Pacific against Japan.

Mr. Bonneau always had some commentary about what he'd read in the daily papers. He reported that the Allied drive toward Germany was still proceeding at a fast pace and, according to the latest news, France was almost entirely liberated. On the eastern front the Russian army was pushing the Nazi forces back. "Mark my words, the Boches are finished! I don't give them more than a month to surrender!" Mr. Bonneau spoke with such assurance and authority that I too was convinced that the end of the war was in sight.

After six weeks with the Bonneaus I had settled into a pleasant routine, splitting my time between school, homework, Boy Scouts and Fernand, my new friend. However, I made sure to use some of my free time to help Mrs. Bonneau. I ran errands in the neighborhood and took her dogs for their daily walk whenever she was not up to it. They were the apples of her eye, and I knew she would appreciate the gesture. I pretended to love the dogs for her sake; but the poodles were not duped by my pretense. They knew instinctively that I didn't care much for them, and returned the sentiment.

Since I'd arrived the poodles kept their distance, probably seeing me as a competitor for their mistress's attention. We had an understanding. I politely greeted them, and they responded with a bark. Whenever I walked them I had a handful trying to keep two high-strung and cunning dogs in line, for they were determined to cause mischief. I kept their leashes tightly wound around my wrist, aware that if they ever broke loose and ran away I would never hear the end of it. As a result I endured the dogs' shenanigans, figuring it was a small price to pay for showing Mrs. Bonneau that I appreciated her kindness.

In a small house voices carry through the walls. For some time I'd heard shouting upstairs that sounded like arguments between Mrs. Bonneau and Madeleine. All along I had done my best to respect their privacy, but it was difficult for me to ignore the tension that had been rising between them, especially when they snapped at each other. Mr. Bonneau, who was usually in charge of the household, seemed to have abdicated his role, at least for the moment, staying away from the squabbling.

In time the argument burst out in the open. Madeleine was in love with a man she'd met at work, and they had decided to get married. She was already considered an old maid at the age of twenty-nine, and this was surely her last chance. When she had asked her parents for their consent to marry this man, Robert Poncelet, they had flatly refused.

The Bonneaus came from a world where marriages were arranged by the parents of the bride. In the past they had hand-picked several prospective husbands, whom Madeleine had rejected. What they really wanted for their daughter was a worldly and wealthy man, not Robert Poncelet, who was just a clerk at a local wine wholesaler where Madeleine was a secretary. Madeleine's sudden burst of independence caught her parents by surprise and created the turmoil, because until now she had been an obedient daughter and most respectful of their wishes. For a while longer there were sharp words exchanged between them. I felt bad to see the rancor and ill feelings among them and tried to stay out of the way.

Eventually the animosity died down, and the Bonneaus consented to meet the man Madeleine had selected. Robert Poncelet came for dinner. It was a tense meeting until Mrs. Bonneau fell under his charm. He was not only handsome, but personable and well-spoken. This first meeting went well, and I heaved a sigh of relief for Madeleine, hoping the Bonneaus would change their minds. There were other meetings. Happily, the Bonneaus relented and finally gave their blessings.

I was glad harmony had finally returned to the Bonneaus' household. Ever since Robert became a frequent dinner guest he had further ingratiated himself with Mr. and Mrs. Bonneau by bringing a couple of fine bottles of wine every time he came over.

By coincidence Robert and his family also belonged to the same Protestant church, a factor which meant a great deal, especially to Mrs. Bonneau. The wedding date was tentatively set for the following summer. Meanwhile Madeleine was basking in her newly found happiness.

16

Vincennes, December 1944

We heard unsettling news over the radio. Apparently the victorious drive toward Germany by Allied forces had been unexpectedly halted by a counter-offensive near Luxembourg, in the densely wooded region of the Ardennes. The first accounts were sketchy. Nonetheless we had to take seriously this last-ditch effort by the Nazis to turn the war around. Although until that moment we felt that victory was at hand, our hopes for a quick ending to the war were suddenly dashed.

With winter knocking at our door, the gray skies overhead and the cold winds were dampening our spirits. Nonetheless, as I walked to school in the early morning, the shivering frost-coated tree branches reminded me of how fortunate I was to be warmly dressed. I was reminded of my sister in Savigny-le-Vieux, and felt sorry for her and wondered how she was faring on the farm as she worked in the cold outdoors.

Since our first letters, more had followed. Both of us looked forward to the day when Mrs. Mounier would be able to bring her back to Vincennes. Sleeping arrangements for Alice would have to be worked out upon her return. A solution was found: she would share Madeleine's bedroom. When I'd arrived, the Bonneaus, with ingenuity, had cleared an alcove upstairs that had previously been used for storage, and managed to squeeze in a bed. With so much effort to find a place for me, I couldn't possibly have taken for granted their extraordinary hospitality. I wondered if any of my parents' other friends would have made such a sacrifice and given up so much of their comfort and privacy for us?

"Simon, I am too busy, please get the front door!" Mrs. Bonneau yelled from the kitchen. I was so absorbed in my homework at the secretary in the parlor that I had not heard the doorbell. I rushed to the door. Two strangers were standing on the doorstep, their faces flushed beet-red from the stinging wind that blew outside. Wearing overcoats and scarves, a short balding middle-aged man and a boy about my age stared at me in an odd way.

I was about to ask them if they were lost or needed directions when the man's face lit up with a broad smile, revealing several gleaming gold teeth. "You must be Zizi!" he exclaimed with a heavy foreign accent, punctuating his statement with a sweeping gesture. I was flabbergasted. How on earth did he know my nickname? Who could that stranger possibly be? As though he'd read my mind the man said, "I am your uncle—David Spiro," then, pointing to the boy at his side, "Raoul—it's your cousin!" I was so overwhelmed by this revelation that I stood transfixed, my heart pounding from the shock.

I slowly regained my composure. "Yes, it's me, Zizi!" I managed to answer. All at once we hugged and kissed. Tears of joy streamed down my cheeks. I was so overcome with happiness that I could hardly wait to share the good news with my sister and brother. Meanwhile our voices had alerted the poodles, who came bounding into the hallway barking ferociously but kept a safe distance from us. Mrs. Bonneau also came rushing to the door and found me excited and smiling in the company of strangers. Like me, she was amazed to learn that they were my uncle and cousin.

I'd assumed that my parents had never told the Bonneaus of the existence of Uncle David and his family. To me he had been only a vague memory, because since I was born he had been the black sheep of our family. I'd never met him before. His name was rarely mentioned at home except when my mother was angry at me for teasing or fighting with Alice. Her last resort to make me stop was to scare me by invoking Uncle David's name. I still could remember her dire warning: "If you don't mend your ways you'll be punished when you grow up, just like my brother, by marrying a witch who will make your life hell!" Suffice it to say that my mother's threats had been enough to make me stop, at least for a while.

Those memories of my childhood rushed back, making me sad

to think that a quarrel had deprived me of knowing my uncle and his family for all those many years until this very moment. Now was my chance to find out for myself who this infamous brother was, the one my mother had loathed so much. But at that moment I was so happy I would have gladly forgiven Uncle David all his past sins. Mrs. Bonneau warmly invited Uncle David and Raoul to come inside to wait for Mr. Bonneau and Madeleine, who were not yet back from work. She served hot tea and biscuits in the parlor. While Mrs. Bonneau and my uncle were busy talking to each other, Raoul and I got acquainted.

Needless to say, Mr. Bonneau and Madeleine were astonished to come home and find two strangers who turned out to be my uncle and cousin. Mr. Bonneau was quite hospitable, insisting that Uncle David and Raoul stay to celebrate this unexpected reunion. We all settled around the dining room table and sipped wine from crystal glasses that Mrs. Bonneau had fetched for this special occasion. Soon the wine began working its magic on us all, making everyone relaxed and gregarious.

Uncle David was asked how he'd managed to survive during the war. He briefly told us how his family had narrowly escaped from the clutches of the police during the early hours of the roundup of July 1942. With his wife and son he had left Paris at once, with only their clothes on their backs, and had fled to the Grand Lucé, a small town in southern Normandy where they had spent many summer vacations in the home of a gentile family. Those people were the only chance they had to escape from the police and the Gestapo. Their prayers were answered. Those brave people not only hid my uncle and aunt with relatives who were farmers, but also took my cousin into their home for the duration of the war.

Just before fleeing Paris, my uncle, who was a watchmaker like my father, had the presence of mind to gather from his workbench all the watches he'd just made and stuff them into his pockets and my aunt's handbag. Those watches turned out to be lifesavers, handy items of barter, for he had little money left. As time went on, the watches became the only way he could possibly compensate the farmers for their food and shelter, and they also ensured their recipients' discretion.

For the next two years Uncle David and his wife, Berthe, lived hidden in a barn, up on the attic floor, where they took their meals and slept. They only came out in the evening or at night, in order to avoid being seen by neighbors.

After my uncle was finished telling his story I reflected on how chance had played such a large part in his survival. This, in turn, painfully reminded me of my parents, whose luck had deserted them.

After the Bonneaus and my uncle retired to the parlor to talk privately I remained with Raoul in the dining-room, happy to be alone with him. My cousin had a pleasant-looking face, roundish, with a thick mop of black hair. He was slightly taller and much heavier than I. As we shared stories about our lives I found him to be quite interesting and articulate, but also somewhat arrogant, displaying a show-off attitude that was annoying. However, at such an early stage of our relationship, I decided to look the other way, hoping that in time we would become good friends.

It was getting late. As Uncle David and Raoul bid the Bonneaus goodbye, I arranged to see them next time in Paris.

My first visit to my newly found relatives was on my day off from school. I took the metro and easily found their house near Place de la Republique. My uncle and aunt lived in a one bedroom apartment on the top floor of an old, run-down four-story building with an outside toilet shared by the tenants. (As I found out later, housing was very scarce in Paris; even a substandard apartment like theirs was only to be had at a steep price.) Narrow, crooked steps with missing tiles led upstairs, exacting constant vigilance to avoid tripping and falling down.

Aunt Berthe let me in. I had not expected to see a witch, as my mother had angrily described her sister-in-law, nor had I anticipated the attractive, refined-looking woman in her early forties with dark hair who opened the door. She hugged me and welcomed me, speaking softly with a slight foreign accent. My uncle and Raoul greeted me warmly as I joined them at a table already set for lunch. With my relatives sitting next to me I almost felt like I was back home *en famille*!

Despite rationing, Aunt Berthe had managed to prepare a delicious lunch. The conversation was flowing, going back and forth between my stories about the past two years in Normandy, about Alice and Michel and their accounts of hiding in the farm, and about Uncle David and Aunt Berthe's tough beginnings after coming back to Paris. I learned how much of a hurdle it had been for them to be able to afford this dingy little apartment with peeling paint and furnished only with the bare essentials. After the liberation, getting work proved to be very difficult. Despite his perseverance, my uncle couldn't get a full-time job. Meanwhile he worked free-lance, repairing watches at home for private customers. He mentioned that he had reconnected with Mr. Friedman and Mr. Pinkowsky, who in the past had used his and my father's services. I remembered them well.

While looking for work after the liberation, my uncle had renewed contact with many Jewish watchmakers he'd known before the war. Most of them belonged to a small tight-knit group of Polish immigrants, including Uncle David and my father, who had settled in Paris and its suburbs. Their conversation had mostly been about business acquaintances who had managed to elude the police and the Gestapo, and those who had been arrested and deported. By coincidence, someone had told him that my parents and their good friends the Krums had been deported.

Uncle David said he was shocked and depressed for weeks as he thought about my parents. "Believe me, I had a fight with your mother a long time ago, and to this day I still regret the incident that caused such rift. I'm sorry we never made up. Afterwards I wondered what had happened to you, to your sister and to your brother. No one knew. Later, another coincidence occurred. I was having a conversation with another watchmaker who had been a close friend of Mr. and Mrs. Krum. He suddenly recalled that after the police roundup, the Krums had come to him to tell him about their plans to go to the non-occupied zone with your parents. They also wanted to make sure that he knew that a gentile family in Vincennes by the name of Bonneau had hidden their son Joseph and the Jeruchims' three children somewhere in Normandy."

Uncle David said that he had been very relieved to learn that Alice, Michel and I had not been deported with our parents. He was determined to find us, and eventually located the Bonneaus. Dramatically thrusting his hands toward me, my uncle recalled the happy day when we met. "You should know that it was the shock of my life when I rang the doorbell and you opened the door! I never expected to find you there. Besides, I never had the opportunity to see you before, even when you were a child. But I knew at once that it was you because of your resemblance to your father."

At last the puzzling circumstances of how Uncle David had suddenly appeared became clear for the first time. It was amazing how a series of coincidences had made it possible for him to find me. How strange were the unexpected twists and turns of life; here was my uncle, the black sheep of the family, ostracized by his sister, who had come forward in a moment of need to help her children. I wistfully wished my mother could have seen from afar her brother's devotion to us. She would have been proud of him!

I asked Uncle David what he thought of the Bonneaus. He went on to give me his impressions of his first visit with them. He felt that they were good and decent people who were very committed to me, Alice and Michel. As they had promised, they had looked after us and would continue to do so until our parents returned from captivity—hopefully soon. Meanwhile they had been trying their best to figure out a way to bring the three of us together. But because of the limited space in their house they could not accommodate Michel. Until a solution was found, they had recommended that he stay with the Leclères until the end of the school year.

While Uncle David was reminiscing, Aunt Berthe occasionally interrupted his soliloquy, reminding him of something that he had forgotten or correcting what she thought was not accurate in his story.

Facing them across the table I was struck by how different they were, almost at opposite poles. Uncle David was animated when he spoke, feisty, giving an occasional chuckle when he thought he'd made a funny remark, his eyes flashing with excitement as a crooked smile twisted his lips. While narrating a story he invariably punctuated his remarks with hand gestures. I felt there was something loveable and impish about him, with his round face, small features and bald dome.

By contrast, Aunt Berthe sat erect, her head high, cool, proper and dignified like *une dame du monde* (a worldly lady), her pretty face conveying little of her emotions. She looked at my uncle with a condescending gaze, as though she merely tolerated his loud emotional outbursts. Still, she occasionally smiled at me to make me feel welcome.

Raoul was not to be denied attention. While his father went on and on with his story, Raoul would yawn or interject rude remarks to provoke him. Uncle David would take the bait and start yelling at Raoul, while Aunt Berthe acted as the referee and managed to quiet things down. I felt terribly uncomfortable having to witness their bickering, and wished that I could vanish.

As I returned to Vincennes I reflected on the emotionally charged couple of weeks since I'd met this family. To have found relatives was a miracle! Even though they weren't perfect, they cared for me enough to have gone out of their way to find me despite pressing concerns of their own in trying to put their lives back together.

As for Raoul, I was determined to overlook his childish outbursts. After all he was my *only* cousin!

18

Vincennes, January 1945

Snow was rare in Vincennes. At most it was an overnight dusting that by morning would melt down to a grayish film of slush. That year, however, winter barreled down on us with angry, icy winds and heavy snows that coated rooftops, streets and sidewalks. Early in the morning, as I walked to school, the frigid weather made me appreciate even more my brand-new woolen gloves, a birthday gift from the Bonneaus.

According to the latest radio news bulletin the severe snowstorm that hit Vincennes had already swept across eastern France, paralyzing the Allied forces massed in the Ardennes. Bad weather and poor visibility were also blamed in part for the Americans' and British forces' lack of success in repelling the powerful Nazi Panzer divisions' counterattack. Meanwhile, heavy fighting was reported all across the front line, an indication that the German army's strength had been grossly underestimated. The latest news was disheartening, and Mr. Bonneau was no longer as optimistic as he'd been in the past.

Despite the latest Allied setback, there were some small improvements in our daily lives. As mail became more reliable, I was happy to learn that my letters were getting to my sister and brother faster. After my initial encounter with Uncle David I set out at once to share the exciting news with Alice and Michel. I only could imagine the expressions on their faces when they read my letters. As I had expected, they wrote back to tell me how stunned they were to learn that we had newly found relatives. They hoped to see them soon.

In addition to the improved postal service, it was also getting easier to travel, although permits were still required for long-distance train trips. Sometime during the middle of January, Mrs.

Bonneau took me completely by surprise. She said that her friend Mrs. Mounier was on her way to Savigny-le-Vieux to bring Alice back to Vincennes, thanks to the two permits she would be able to secure. I could hardly believe that it was finally happening. From that time on I impatiently counted the hours and minutes.

Several days later I returned from school and Mrs. Bonneau let me into the house. It was quiet inside except for the familiar sound of the grandfather clock ticking away and a couple of barks from the poodles greeting my arrival. I wondered how Mrs. Bonneau had managed to keep a straight face when she led me to the parlor where Alice and Mrs. Mounier were waiting for me. I walked right into the trap, and even though I'd been preparing myself for this very moment I felt like I was dreaming the whole thing.

After my initial shock Alice and I ran into each other's arms, kissing and laughing at the same time, relief freely pouring out from our hearts. It had been about four months since we were together. At last I was reunited with my sister, her face still glowing with rosy cheeks acquired from the outdoors around the farm, and I was ecstatic. Mrs. Mounier also embraced me. She was still the same attractive woman I remembered from Savigny-le-Vieux, pert-looking with blond hair framing her pretty face.

Later Mr. Bonneau and Madeleine were also pleasantly surprised to find my sister and Mrs. Mounier at home. After dinner we spent the evening relaxing around the dining room table and talking about their trip. Mrs. Mounier recalled when she met Alice and me for the first time in the Bonneaus' house, and when she took us to Savigny-le-Vieux in the fall of 1942. Was it possible that it had been just a little more than two years since we fled to Normandy? It seemed like another era.

Even though the topic at hand was rather serious, Mrs. Mounier managed to liven up the conversation with humorous remarks and even succeeded in making Mr. Bonneau roar with laughter—not a small feat, considering his rather staid personality.

After my sister settled into the day-to-day routine and adjusted to the Bonneaus' ways, Mrs. Bonneau helped her apply to the Lycée de Vincennes, a private school she'd attended before. Alice's application was accepted, and soon she was able to resume her schooling. But the first thing she wanted, more than anything else, was to meet our uncle, and aunt and cousin. On our day off from school we took the metro to Paris. I led my sister to where they lived on Rue Aumaire, a twisting cobblestone street lined with small, decaying apartment houses. When we entered the building Alice became nervous. We climbed up to the fourth floor where Uncle David, Aunt Berthe and Raoul were waiting on the landing to greet us. They, too, had been impatiently looking forward to meeting my sister. It was a very emotional reunion, with many hugs and joyful tears. Aunt Berthe had prepared a festive lunch for us to celebrate the occasion. I noticed that since my last visit the apartment looked cozier, brighter. I realized that the walls had been repainted in a pleasing pastel shade of blue, the wooden floor had been freshly waxed and new curtains hid the old, peeling window frames.

I imagined that Aunt Berthe had had a hand in such a nice transformation. From the first time I met her she had struck me as a proud woman determined to keep her dignity and, despite hard times, she refused to live in squalor. Clearly my aunt cared very much about appearances, and like a drill sergeant she enforced a strict dress code for her family. She practiced what she preached and was always well-groomed and tastefully attired for her guests. As for Uncle David and Raoul, she made them wear jackets and ties, even at home. I felt it was just a matter of time until she made me follow her rules.

For lunch Aunt Berthe had prepared a brisket with roasted potatoes and sour pickles, reminding me of my mother's cooking, a mixture of Jewish and French recipes. I enjoyed this delectable meal, and the delicious flavor of brisket and sour pickles brought back warm memories of my childhood and of a time when my mother, Alice and I traveled to the Jewish neighborhood of Paris to buy corned beef, hot dogs, pickles and smoked fish. The delicatessen was an emporium of wonderful Jewish specialty foods that invaded my senses with mouth-watering smells.

Alice was clearly enjoying herself, happy to be the center of attention and busy answering questions posed by Uncle David and Aunt Berthe. For once Raoul was on his best behavior and almost deferential toward my sister, possibly impressed that she went to a Lycée, which compared to public schools had a certain panache. At one point during the conversation, Alice wondered if there was any chance Michel would be back with us soon. "I wish I could find a way to make it happen," Uncle David responded. "But now you must be patient. As you know, I had to agree with Mr. and Mrs. Bonneau's decision to keep him with the Leclères until the end of the school year." He added in a confidential tone of voice, "Besides, there are still financial matters to be worked out," not bothering to elaborate. I felt it would be impolite to press him for more explanations. On our way back to Vincennes Alice was walking on air, still excited from having seen our newly found relatives. "It's a miracle that they found us!" she exclaimed.

Vincennes, April 1945

Winter's icy mantle and mournful skies finally gave way to the return of spring. Balmy weather and blue skies once again cast their magic upon us. Trees were in full bloom along the avenues and in the Bois de Vincennes, my favorite park, where my father had taught me how to ride my first bike. The pleasant weather seemed to make everything better. People were more relaxed, smiling again, especially with the latest uplifting news that the war might soon be over.

We breathed a deep sigh of relief when we learned that the bloody winter battle in the Ardennes had been decisively won by the Allies. After crushing the powerful Panzer divisions, the Germans' last hope to derail the invasion, the Americans and British had been able to attack Germany on its own soil. At the same time other news reports indicated that Russian troops were within striking distance of Berlin's suburbs.

My brother's birthday was in April. I wished Alice and I could have been with him to celebrate his eighth birthday! He often asked the same question: When would he be able to see us again? We wrote to him as often as possible, trying to reassure him that we would soon be reunited. It was not easy to explain the complexity of life to an eight-year-old boy. Meanwhile he kept us abreast of his daily life and schoolwork, proudly mailing us his excellent report cards.

Since my sister returned to Vincennes our homework seemed to take up much of our free time. Nonetheless I managed to attend Boy Scout reunions and continued to see Fernand, though less often than in the past. For her part, Alice had struck up a friendship with several girls at the Lycée de Vincennes, and from time to time she met with them.

I couldn't help but feel envious of my sister, who seemed to breeze through her schoolwork and get excellent results, while I worked harder but only managed passing marks in math and sciences. Of course I was disappointed, but more so for Mr. Bonneau, who had appointed himself my tutor and mentor. "Only the best will do!" he admonished me. Unbeknownst to me, he had already set goals for me.

Mr. Bonneau said he'd been thinking about my future. When he asked me what I had in mind, I told him my fondest dream was to become a commercial artist someday. He immediately rejected my choice as foolishness. "My dear boy, at best it would be a nice hobby, but it is not a profession," he chuckled. He said he had already decided that I should study to become an engineer, adding with passion in his voice, "As you know, I have worked as an engineer for many years, and I can tell you with pride that it's a noble and rewarding profession that has served me well. In time you'll thank me."

My heart sank when I heard this. I was dismayed. How could he ignore my obvious lack of aptitude for math and sciences? To contradict him would have been inconceivable, because in those days an adult always had the last word. Mr. Bonneau most likely had my welfare in mind in making such a decision; but I wondered whether he had been blinded by his desire to have me follow in his footsteps.

I had no choice but to comply. I learned with growing apprehension that I was scheduled to take a test for admission to the Diderot Technical School in May.

19

Vincennes, May 1945
The once-formidable Nazi war machine was near collapse. We counted the days and kept our fingers crossed, hoping the end was near. Newspapers reported with bold headlines, "Berlin Has Fallen" and that Allied forces were closing in on victory. Nevertheless we remained apprehensive, not ready to celebrate until it was official.

It was May 7 when the much-anticipated radio broadcast announced the total surrender of Nazi Germany to the Allies. The news spread like wildfire. I was in school when my teacher told us that he'd just heard that the war was over. There was stunned silence for a brief moment, then cheers erupted, followed by catcalls and laughter. Soon total pandemonium had taken over. Kids began jumping on desks. Others threw pencils and notebooks across the room. The teacher tried in vain to restore order. I was overcome by feelings of joy and relief, which brought to heart the renewed hope that my parents might be soon liberated from the Nazi labor camps of Eastern Europe.

Schools were closed to mark the end of the war in Europe. Alice and I were thrilled to have some time off to celebrate together such a wonderful and historic moment in our lives. Mr. Bonneau had invited some friends over for a little gathering and opened some of his best bottles of wine, which he'd saved for this occasion. We all toasted the Allied victory. I probably had too much to drink, because the full-bodied vintage Bordeaux went straight to my head. I panicked when everything around me began spinning like a merry-go-round, but luckily I managed to stay on my feet.

A festive mood permeated our entire neighborhood as though everyone was eager to share his happiness with strangers. Passersby smiled and greeted each other like old friends. Street parties took place everywhere under canopies of streamers and flags hung from lampposts. The most memorable event that week was the victory rally held at the Vincennes city hall.

On a beautiful spring day the Bonneaus, Alice and I joined a happy crowd milling around in the square in front of the ornate facade of the imposing Vincennes city hall, draped with the French colors of bright streaks of blue, white and red flapping in the gentle breeze. When we arrived a French military band was assembled on a platform erected along the city hall steps, playing rousing marches while people sang along. Meanwhile many dignitaries wearing tricolor sashes and men in uniform took their places on chairs around a podium.

Suddenly clapping and shouts of *"Vive de Gaulle!"* rang through the squares as the general himself made a grand entrance, marching behind an honor guard carrying banners bearing the cross of Lorraine (a symbol worn by French partisans during the occupation). De Gaulle stood on the platform, in dress uniform, a tall and lanky figure. He then began waving his arms, acknowledging the noisy ovation from people who chanted in unison *"Vive de Gaulle! Vive de Gaulle! Vive de Gaulle!"*

The general delivered a rousing patriotic speech, interrupted many times by the cheering and appreciative crowd. It reminded me of when le Père Geslin clandestinely listened to Radio London to hear de Gaulle speak to Frenchmen. There was no doubt in my mind that de Gaulle had been a beacon of light during the darkest hours of the war, keeping hope alive that one day the Nazis would be defeated. I couldn't help but feel awed by his towering presence. Afterward the band played "La Marseillaise," our stirring national anthem, and the crowd sang along.

The next day Alice and I visited our uncle, aunt and cousin, and together we went to the Champs Elysées, where victory celebrations were still taking place. From the metro we ran into a noisy sea of humanity overflowing onto the sidewalks, standing shoulder to shoulder to catch a glimpse of the military parades marching down the avenue.

Some daring individuals climbed lampposts and trees for better vantage points. We didn't get to see much of the parades, but we didn't really mind. We had a great time listening to the bands and being part of the celebration, as people walked arm in arm singing and waving flags.

Eventually the school holiday was over and the day arrived when I took the test for admission to Diderot Technical High School. Several weeks later I went to check the results posted at the entrance to the school. Alas, I hadn't passed the test. I felt devastated, but more for Mr. Bonneau's sake than my own.

As I had expected, Mr. Bonneau was furious when he learned that I'd failed. He stopped talking to me. Mrs. Bonneau and Madeleine did their best to appease him, but he remained angry with me for quite a while.

Mr. Bonneau stubbornly refused to let the issue rest and asked Uncle David to come over "to discuss a matter of grave importance," as he phrased it. I had already told my uncle that I'd failed a test.

To my great relief, Uncle David had taken the news with equanimity and offered some advice: "Look, Zizi, it's not the worst thing in the world to fail a test. So maybe you won't become an engineer like Mr. Bonneau wanted, but you can always learn to be a watchmaker like me and your father. It's not only a fine profession, but I can assure you that you'll never go hungry!"

Mr. Bonneau didn't mince his words during the meeting with my uncle. In front of me he told him that since I'd failed that test, I was basically a failure without any prospect of success. I was terribly embarrassed and shocked to hear such harsh words from Mr. Bonneau, who in the past struck me as strict but fair. Could it be that his bitterness had clouded his judgment? I was grateful to Uncle David, who came to my defense and argued that a fifteen-year-old boy, no matter the circumstances, had a full life still ahead.

As the discussion continued the earlier civility between them was touched with rancor. No conclusion was reached during this meeting; but Uncle David intimated to Mr. Bonneau that he had some ideas of his own for my future, which he would discuss with him at an appropriate time. The goodbyes were polite but curt when my uncle finally left. I couldn't help but feel terribly guilty that I had caused such a rift between them.

Vincennes, June 1945

I was relieved that Mr. Bonneau never again mentioned the test or the incident with my uncle. Yet I sensed some coolness toward me. Perhaps he still felt hurt that I would never follow in his footsteps. At the same time I was doing quite well in school, ready to calm my stern critic with my good grades.

Meanwhile Alice and I continued our periodic visits to our uncle and aunt. During one of those pleasant get-togethers Uncle David revealed what he had planned for our future. What he said took us completely by surprise. Alice and I were startled to learn that for the past couple months he and Aunt Berthe had been looking for ways to reunite Michel with us. At last they'd found a solution. As my uncle once more explained to us, bringing our brother back to Vincennes wasn't possible: for one thing, the Bonneaus didn't have enough room; for another, they simply couldn't afford to care for another child.

Uncle David's "solution" left Alice and me speechless! We nervously looked at each other when he told us that with the aid of a Jewish organization all three of us soon would be relocated to a children's home outside of Paris. Apparently Alice's expression and mine betrayed our shock and consternation. Uncle David was quick to point out the three of us would be together again. One revelation followed another when he added that he had recently become our official guardian, and therefore the Bonneaus could not oppose his decision. Yet there were more surprises in Uncle David's bag of tricks! He and Aunt Berthe and Raoul had been planning a two-week vacation in July, back to the town in Normandy where they had been hidden during the war. Alice and I would be included, and Michel too. I'd never expected such a wonderful surprise! My mind reeled under the barrage of so many disclosures as I tried to sort out how these changes would affect our lives.

Vincennes, July 1945

The school year finally was over. Alice and I were pleased that we had successfully completed all our courses. With some sadness we recognized that it would be our last school year in Vincennes, but we chose not to mention it to the Bonneaus. It was up to my uncle to inform them of his decision concerning our future.

Shortly after our graduation Uncle David and Aunt Berthe came to Vincennes. The Bonneaus received them cordially. It was the first time that Aunt Berthe had met them, and with her refined manners she instantly won them over. We all sat in the dining room munching on pastries over pleasant small talk, until Uncle David came to the heart of the matter. The Bonneaus obviously had not expected to hear that Alice and I would be leaving them. They were very upset. Uncle David made it clear that he was our legal guardian and that everything he did was in our best interest. I felt sorry for the Bonneaus, who had done so much for us and perhaps felt betrayed.

From that time on the atmosphere between the Bonneaus and us was strained, especially with Mr. Bonneau, who was aloof and distant from us. Mrs. Bonneau and Madeleine were more understanding, realizing that Alice and I had no say in the matter. I felt terribly sad having to leave that way, especially since they had done so much for us. We all shed tears when Alice and I said goodbye.

We traveled with Aunt Berthe and Raoul to le Grand Lucée in Normandy. In the meantime Uncle David had returned from St. Aubin-les-Elbeuf with my brother. How can I express the joy Alice and I felt when we saw Michel, three long years after I left him with the Leclère family?

My first vision: There he was standing in front of us, a slender, cute eight-year-old boy wearing short pants, with a shy smile brightening his face. His first words were *"Bonjour, Monsieur Zizi, bonjour, Mademoiselle Alice."* We would have none of such formality. We squeezed Michel to us, vowing to never let him go!

Children's Homes

20

Cailly-sur-Eure, Summer 1945
We spent two wonderful carefree weeks in the pastoral country town of Le Grand Lucée. Despite my earlier qualms, I got along well with Raoul and had a good time at the nearby community pool, where Alice, Michel and I took swimming lessons. During our vacation Alice and I had many opportunities to get closer to Michel and bridge the gap of our long separation. After a couple of days his initial reticence disappeared. Instead I was glad to discover that my brother was an active and somewhat mischievous eight-year-old boy.

After our vacation Alice, Michel and I returned to Paris and briefly stayed with Uncle David and Aunt Berthe until we left for the children's home. I'd been thinking about this new home with some anxiety, wondering what the future held in store for us. Aunt Berthe said she was told I would have an opportunity there to learn a good trade, such as an electrician or tailor. I was upset by the notion that I would never have a chance to become an artist, but I was realistic enough to accept the fact that my desire was only a pipe dream.

My aunt had been aware all along of how much I wanted to become an artist, and like Mr. Bonneau she was of the opinion that it was a foolish idea. Reading the disappointment in my face she declared, "Mark my words, Zizi, one day you'll thank me for not letting you become one of those starving homeless artists sleeping under the bridges of the Seine River!"

Alice, Michel and I traveled to the sleepy little town of Cailly-sur-Eure in Normandy, a couple of hours by train from Paris. The children's home was an old mansion with a steep slate roof and tall chimneys, located on sprawling grounds along the Eure River bank next to a bridge. When we arrived, workmen were finishing renovations outside and painting walls inside. We spent the following week learning our way around, meeting the other children and staff and trying to familiarize ourselves with the rules and daily routine of the home.

We had joined dozens of other Jewish boys and girls from the age of eight to eighteen. Some had arrived before us; many more were yet to come. We were painfully aware that we had a common bond uniting us: each of us had parents who had been deported during the war.

We were split into groups according to age and gender. My brother was assigned with *les petits* (the youngsters), while my sister and I were placed with *les grands* (the teenagers). We slept in improvised dormitories, partitioned to keep boys and girls apart.

The children's home was run by a friendly and cheerful couple in their late thirties by the name of Cohn-Bendit, German Jews who had managed to escape the Nazis. My counselor was Ernest, a German Jewish refugee who commanded instant respect with his barrel-chest, crew cut, piercing blue eyes and jutting chin. He wore several hats, supervising all outdoor activities and sports, enforcing discipline during meals and sounding curfew and reveille with the shiny whistle that always hung from his neck.

At night Ernest snuck into our dormitory. Anyone caught making noise was punished with extra chores the next day. After his wake-up call, Ernest was back minutes later. Anyone lingering in bed was unceremoniously dumped on the floor with the mattress on top of him. Needless to say, Ernest made an impression on us, especially when he barked orders in his heavy German accent. We called him Boche behind his back.

Fortunately other counselors were kinder than him. For instance there was Mr. Horowitz, a man in his early forties who taught electronics and Hebrew. His friendly demeanor inspired me to become an electrician instead of a tailor. There were about a dozen boys who opted to take his course, which was held twice a week in an abandoned horse stable. In this unlikely classroom, several workbenches with tools had been set among stalls. The lessons contained some theory, but mostly covered practical applications like splicing and connecting wiring to the outlets, switches and fuse boxes found around the stable.

I was perplexed to discover on one of the interior stone walls that had recently been whitewashed, a mural showing an eagle with wings widespread holding a swastika still visible through the whitewash. I later learned that the mansion had been requisitioned during the war by Nazis and until the liberation had served as a garrison. It was ironic, I thought, that a year later Jewish children would find shelter in a place formerly occupied by their worst enemy!

Mr. Horowitz asked whether any of us were familiar with Hebrew and also had the artistic dexterity needed to decorate the dining hall walls with the text of a Hebrew song. I eagerly volunteered for the job, confident I could copy the intricate letterforms Mr. Horowitz had shown us in a book. I went to work perched on a ladder in order to be able to reach the top of the walls. I proceeded by carefully outlining each letter in pencil and then going over it with paint, aware that Mr. Horowitz was silently scrutinizing my work.

By the time I had finished my assignment, with Mr. Horowitz's help, I was able to read the words of this popular song: *"Hinei ma tov uma na'im, shevet achim gam yachad,"* which translated meant "Behold, how good and how pleasant it is, when brethren dwell together in unity."

The graceful shapes of the letters I'd painted on the walls reminded me of how little I knew about my Jewish heritage. All along I had been trying to distance myself from a foreign culture in which I felt I had no part. This was the first time I felt some sense of pride in being Jewish, and I wondered whether a mysterious link connected those Hebrew words with my parents' past and the world of their ancestors in Poland?

In my mind, my awakening toward Judaism had little to do with God or religion, but rather with the need to come to terms with the Jewish identity I'd worked so hard to keep hidden during the war, from others and also from myself.

Several days later I had completed my project, notwithstanding several close calls during which I courted disaster, almost tipping over the paint can from the top of the ladder and smearing freshly painted letters.

I was relieved when, after examining my work, Mr. Horowitz's face lit up and he shook my hand. After breakfast Dr. Cohn-Bendit and the counselors told the assembled children about the day's activities. After the announcements the director called the kids' attention to my artwork around the dining hall walls and thanked me for my contribution. I was glowing with pleasure, especially to be complimented in front of Alice and Michel and applauded by the other children and the staff.

Soon all the kids were split up into teams and took turns cleaning and helping in the kitchen. Otherwise we were free to participate in organized activities around the grounds, such as soccer, volleyball, swimming or even hiking along the towering limestone cliffs facing the River Eure on the far side of the bridge.

During one of those hikes on top of the cliffs we came upon several graves, just about in line with the bridge. We were told by people in the village that local partisans had been killed at that very spot by German fire while trying to ambush a convoy passing below. It was a reminder of how the war had touched so many people, even in this little village.

Even though we had many books and magazines available to us in the home, we seldom had access to newspapers or radio. The only radio was in the director's office, and periodically Mr. Cohn-Bendit kept us abreast of important news. Sometime at the beginning of August he told us during the usual morning announcements that American planes had dropped "atomic bombs" on Japan and destroyed entire cities. I imagined that no one among us had the faintest idea of the meaning of "atomic bomb," except perhaps for Mr. Horowitz, who was an engineer. Anyway, according to that startling radio newscast "those new terrifying weapons of war might force Japan into surrender sooner than expected."

The summer months went quickly by, the Bonneaus already receding into the past. I had written several letters, but had not gotten any reply. Did they hold a grudge against me, I wondered? I had given up hearing from the Bonneaus when I received a cheerful letter from Madeleine, in which she wrote how happy she was, recently married to Robert Poncelet and living with him in a small apartment they'd found in Vincennes. I was relieved to at least hear from her. She told me not to worry about her parents, feeling they would eventually come around and respond to my letters. However, she knew they were still smarting from our sudden departure and hated my uncle for having taken us away.

I also wrote to Uncle David, Aunt Berthe and Raoul and was happy to read that they were planning to see us at the end of the summer. Aunt Berthe said she was pleased that I was applying myself toward my future profession of electrician.

Living in the children's home was like belonging to a large family. We had to share everything, and everyone counted on us to carry out whatever chores were assigned to us. The food was a far cry from the delicious cooking of Mrs. Bonneau or Aunt Berthe, but it filled our bellies and we never left the table hungry. There was a friendly and happy ambiance in the home, and I imagined a stranger would have been hard put to guess we all were children of the Holocaust.

Curiously, no one ever alluded to the past. We were willing to talk about anything else, but otherwise kept our pains and memories locked inside our hearts. On the outside there were no scars to be seen. We behaved like typical kids of our ages, at times rambunctiously and mercilessly teasing each other. The bond we felt with each other helped us to form friendships.

In my group there were two boys of about my age with whom I became quite close. Sami was one of them, outgoing and funny. He was tall and skinny, all arms and legs, with curly red hair jutting above his face full of freckles. Michel, my other friend, was the opposite, short and rather shy. Nonetheless, as different as we were the three of us became an inseparable trio. My sister also became fast friends with a girl named Rachel. As for my brother, he seemed to have found kids he liked, especially a boy named Gaby, who was one of the director's sons.

21

Cailly-sur-Eure, Fall 1945

In time, traditions and special Jewish holidays became a part of our daily lives in the home, even though most kids, like me were unfamiliar with Jewish rituals and never went to a synagogue. At first I felt uneasy having to learn and recite Hebrew prayers; but eventually I came to accept and even enjoy the casual family atmosphere in which the religion played a part.

We were taught to recite blessings before and after each meal and to participate in the Friday night Sabbath service. The Sabbath was observed in the dining hall, scrubbed for the weekly ritual and decorated with freshly-laundered tablecloths and flowers. We, too, had to look our best for this occasion, in clean white shirts, with our hair combed and shoes shined. Ernest made sure everyone followed the rules. Dr. Cohn-Bendit led the informal service, which was followed by lively singing of some Hebrew folk songs that Mr. Horowitz had taught us. After a while I began looking forward to those weekly Jewish rituals.

During that time I turned to Mr. Horowitz, seeking to learn more about the Jewish religion out of curiosity. He was pleased. He knew that, like most kids in the home, I had no prior Jewish education. He had a long talk with me during which he brought up the topic of the Bar Mitzvah and its significance. With his arm around my shoulders he looked me in the eyes to emphasize how special this right of passage was for Jewish males reaching their thirteenth birthdays. "Well, I suppose it's over for me, because I am already fifteen," I replied. Mr. Horowitz said there was actually no age limit for the Bar Mitzvah, and if I wished, even at my age I still could make this important contract with God. Even though I was not in the least religious, I impulsively agreed to go through with it.

When I told my sister she didn't try to dissuade me, even though she couldn't quite understand my sudden transformation. "What about Uncle and Aunt? Should you let them know?" Alice wondered out loud. I had thought of telling them about my plans, but knowing Uncle David's communist leanings, I thought he would scoff at my decision. Besides, at that stage I was not aware that a Bar Mitzvah was an important ceremony to be attended by family, relatives and friends. I had the erroneous notion that my Bar Mitzvah would only consist of a few prayers in the presence of Dr. Cohn-Bendit and a couple of witnesses.

The process was not as simple as I'd imagined. I spent many weeks being coached by Mr. Horowitz in preparation for my Bar Mitzvah, and had to memorize and chant in Hebrew many prayers and my portion of the Torah. The boys in my group had no interest in such religious pursuits, except Sami, who, inspired by my zeal, decided to follow suit.

The day finally arrived. It was a simple ceremony held in the dining hall, officiated by Dr. Cohn-Bendit. Everyone in the home was there, including several women I'd never seen before. Later I learned they were important members of the Woman International Zionist Organization, the American-Jewish organization that sponsored our home.

Sami and I managed to recite the prayers and the Torah portion of the Torah without too many grievous mistakes. The mistakes we made were graciously overlooked by Mr. Horowitz, who helped us through the more difficult passages. We were both relieved when it finally was over. We gratefully acknowledged the congratulations, kisses, handshakes and gifts, such as a book of Jewish songs from Mr. Horowitz, fountain pen from Dr. Cohn-Bendit and a wallet filled with money from the ladies of the WIZO. It was indeed a very exciting moment. I felt like I belonged.

In October Michel and the other kids his age attended the elementary school in Cailly-sur-Eure, a short distance on foot from the home. I was glad he could continue his schooling. For Alice and me and the boys and girls our age, on the other hand there was no way to advance our education in such a small town. There was no high school, nor even a middle school. I really couldn't complain, for I was taught a trade; but no provisions were made to teach my sister and the other girls in her group any trades or special skills. They looked after the younger kids or performed housekeeping chores. However, there was enough spare time left for Alice to read, a pastime she adored. Fortunately for her, books were readily available in the home.

As for me, I continued honing my skills in electrical work, laying out circuits under Mr. Horowitz's vigilant eye. Between lessons I often made little sketches in my notebook. One day Mr. Horowitz, becoming aware that I was drawing, took a look at them. "They are very good indeed," he said. "You have talent that shouldn't be wasted!" This was high praise coming from Mr. Horowitz. Several days later he said that Dr. Cohn-Bendit had approved a project he had in mind for me, namely, to paint a mural in the dining hall on a biblical theme. I was enormously flattered, but also left wondering if I possibly could meet such challenge.

The biblical theme Mr. Horowitz chose was the crossing of the Red Sea. I sketched many ideas on paper to get his approval before proceeding with the mural. One sketch was a whimsical depiction of Jews driving Jeeps between the parted waves of the Red Sea, chased by Egyptian soldiers on motorcycles wearing German helmets. I showed it to Mr. Horiwitz, but strictly as a joke. He had a big laugh over it and showed it to Dr. Cohn-Bendit. He, too, roared with laughter, but to my great surprise he selected it over the more traditional biblical representations I would have expected him to choose.

My next task was to adapt the sketch into a large mural on one of the walls. Little by little the painting took shape under the scrutiny of curious kids who stopped by, looked over my shoulder and gawked at me while I applied colors. From a distance the mural suddenly came alive, with bold strokes of blue and aqua leaping over each other shaping the walls of water, and within, a convoy of jeeps reaching the other side. I had never expected such results and so many compliments!

The world was finally at peace. War in Europe had ended back in May, and Japan surrendered in August. In the waning days of the war I still held hope for my parents' return. But now we were hearing heart-wrenching stories about the horrific conditions in the death camps from people who had made it back to Paris.

This was the first time we heard such accounts, and they shattered our notion that deported Jews had been sent to labor camps. There were rumors that Jews who had been liberated by Russian troops were sent to Russia and held in camps there. The news was bad, but I clung to my hope for a miracle.

Cailly-sur-Eure, December 1945

Uncle David, Aunt Berthe and Raoul visited us during the Christmas holidays. Alice, Michel and I were overjoyed. It was an event to have one's relatives greeted by Dr. Cohn-Bendit, Mr. Horowitz and the other counselors. We introduced our relatives to our friends. Aunt Berthe had brought us some chocolate and a cake with raisins that she had baked. We ate together in the dining hall, and I proudly pointed out my mural on the wall and the inscription in Hebrew around the room. I thought Raoul was impressed for once, his mouth gaping.

Uncle David was relieved that Alice, Michel and I did not complain about the home. "It was not an easy decision for me and your aunt to send you away," he said, "but I'm glad it all worked out for the best." Before going back home Aunt Berthe gave me a little package and told me to open it later. "It's your birthday present," she said with a smile. It was a box filled with an assortment of colored pencils.

Cailly-sur-Eure, Spring 1946

Time passed a lot more quickly among my new friends and the extended family of the children's home. Another season had quickly gone by. Luckily it had been a mild winter without snow, just rain and some occasional slush under foot. Outside the mansion a sudden invasion of dandelions sprinkled the grass with bright yellow flakes, welcoming the early spring and Passover. We read the Haggadah together, leaning comfortably on pillows the way our ancestors did. Michel took part by asking one of the four traditional questions. The ceiling of the dining hall was draped with sheets, giving the appearance of a huge tent. We read, sang, sipped red wine and munched matzoh. It was a most joyous celebration, and poignantly reflected our own escape and fortunate liberation.

Cailly-sur-Eure, May 1946

Mr. Horowitz told our class that we had done well mastering the basics, and soon we all would qualify as assistant electricians. It was gratifying to hear that we had reached the first level of our future trade. I had to remember to inform Uncle David and Aunt Berthe of my progress.

Then Mr. Horowitz took me aside. "I have some exciting news I need to discuss with you," he said with a grin on his face. He told me that even though I had the aptitude to become a fine electrician, he felt that it would be a shame to waste the special artistic talent I had demonstrated in the home. "I've located an excellent art school in Paris that awards scholarships for gifted students. You must take a test to qualify, but I have no doubt that you will succeed."

I was stunned and speechless upon hearing such incredible news. Mr. Horowitz's proposition had been my dream all along. But how could I expect to realize it without financial help and a place to stay? And even if I was to pass the test and earn a scholarship, my uncle's and aunt's blessings would be needed.

When I finally regained my composure and told Mr. Horowitz about the hurdles I faced, he waved his hand as though to sweep away all my concerns. "You need not worry yet, just take the test. I promise to help you and talk to your uncle and aunt," he said cheerfully. How could I possibly let such a wonderful opportunity pass? I nervously accepted the challenge.

When I told my sister about my plans, hoping for her support, she reacted cautiously. I really could not blame her for voicing concerns I had felt myself. Nonetheless, the die was cast. I was determined to go ahead with my plan, hoping that it was not a foolish enterprise. Toward the end of May I left for Paris to take the test.

It had been almost a year since my last visit to Paris, and I rediscovered the frantic pace of big-city life, with traffic, horns blaring, busy streets, crowded sidewalks and people rushing about. I easily located the art school near the Temple metro stop. I was disappointed to come upon a drab-looking four-story brick building that spanned an entire block, hardly the aesthetic structure I'd imagined for an art center. Carved words above the entrance read *Ecole des Arts Appliqués.*

I joined dozens of boys my age in a large hall, and we found our places as assigned desks. The lengthy test consisted of a short academic quiz and an art project, for which we were given more time. Afterwards, even though I was confident I'd done well, I didn't dare speculate about the outcome of the test, afraid to jinx myself. I was told the results would be mailed to us.

Several weeks of intolerable suspense followed until I received the long-awaited letter. With trembling hands I slipped the single sheet of paper from the envelope, looking for the answer that would determine my entire future. There it was, in carefully written script. It began, "Dear Mr. Jeruchim: We are pleased...." The words "We are pleased" danced and flashed on the page before my eyes.

So it was true, I'd passed the test! The anxiety I'd felt for the past couple of weeks instantly vanished. I continued reading the letter, finding that not only had I passed the entrance examination, I had won a scholarship. I could hardly believe such luck. The letter ended by reminding me that I was enrolled in the school for the fall semester.

I ran to show the letter to my sister. Alice was thrilled by my good fortune, but I felt my spirits sag when she later admonished me that I should have thought to ask Uncle David's and Aunt Berthe's permission. I was afraid that she was right. However, Mr. Horowitz, by contrast, was jubilant and confident that he would rally my uncle and aunt to his side.

True to his promise, Mr. Horowitz went to Paris to talk to them. Upon his return I was heartened by his smiling expression. He nearly shouted, "I have your uncle's and aunt's permission. You can rest easy!" I gave a deep sigh of relief because my uncle and aunt were not easy people to persuade if they felt otherwise. Mr. Horowitz continued, "I told them exactly why you took the test and made sure they knew you were not to be blamed."

Another major hurdle still to be negotiated was finding another home where I could stay, within commuting distance of the school.

Dr. Cohn-Bendit took pains to locate such home. The search was made difficult by the fact that not all children's homes in the suburbs around Paris were subsidized by the same American-Jewish organization.

Fortunately Dr. Cohn-Bendit, through his personal contacts, placed me in a home in Rueil-Malmaison, a northwest suburb of Paris, and arranged my transfer in late September, before school started. I couldn't have asked for more, yet I knew that later I would have to pay a price, leaving behind Alice, Michel and kids with whom I'd formed close friendships.

22

Rueil-Malmaison, Fall 1946

The train sped toward Paris across the picturesque Normandy countryside. Every mile brought me closer to the new children's home
and to the promise of a new beginning. As Cailly-sur-Eure receded
into my past I felt my heart caught on a rollercoaster of emotions,
saddened that I would be no longer with Alice and Michel, yet excited that my dream of going to art school was a reality.

I saw my uncle and aunt on my way to the children's home. This
gave me an opportunity to make sure they were no longer upset
with me for taking matters into my own hands. I pressed the buzzer
with trepidation, bracing myself for a chilly reception. Instead I was
pleasantly surprised by their warm welcome. Uncle David said I had
Mr. Horowitz to thank for convincing him. "He persuaded your
aunt that you had the talent and determination to succeed," he said.
Aunt Berthe chimed in, "I agree with your uncle, but I am still worried whether you'll be able to earn a decent living as an artist."

I was relieved that my uncle and aunt were finally reconciled
with my future plans, and I was pleased to hear Mr. Horowitz's
glowing words about me. With my relatives' warm support I felt as
though I was ready to conquer the world. Even my cousin Raoul
was excited at the prospect of seeing each other more often, since I
would be closer to Paris.

Traveling by subway and bus I arrived at Rueil-Malmaison, a
suburb of Paris about half an hour northwest of the city. The home
was an imposing graystone house set back from the street behind tall
walnut trees.

I met the director, Dr. Wexler, a short, compact, energetic-looking
middle-aged woman with a crinkly grin that lit up her face. She didn't
waste time showing me around. She briskly led me through the

rambling two-story mansion to the bedroom I was to share with other boys.

She told me that there were about forty young men and women in the home between eighteen and twenty-one years old. They all worked, many at jobs in the garment district in Paris. Dr. Wexler said she'd made an exception to take me in, only as a favor to Dr. Cohn-Bendit, who had interceded on my behalf. She explained that the Jewish organization sponsoring the home had not made any provision for younger students. While close supervision was not needed as at Cailly-sur-Eure, there were rules everyone had to follow, she said, such as observing curfew and respecting each other's privacy.

After a couple of weeks it became apparent to me that the home was vastly different from the one in Cailly-sur-Eure, where a communal life prevailed. By contrast, everyone here was on his own, since there were no organized activities. Other striking differences were the absence of the Jewish customs I had become used to, like Friday night services, holiday observances or even simple blessings at meals. Dinner was a casual affair, served buffet-style to accommodate those coming home late from work.

The young men and women in the home seemed like adults, although some were not much older than I, in part because of the way they dressed and their streetsmart ways. In the evening some gathered downstairs to play cards, chess or other games, but most engaged in heated political discussions under a thick haze of cigarette smoke. Some girls, probably wanting to appear older and more sophisticated, wore bright red lipstick and rouge and openly flirted with the boys. All of it was quite new to me, like discovering another world.

I had two roommates, Jean-Marc and Pierre, both about twenty and easygoing, except when they quarreled about politics and were at each other's throat. They were at opposite ends of the political spectrum. Jean-Marc was convinced that communism was a tool of repression, while Pierre argued that it was the only just social system for the working man. Each tried to pull me to his side. Jean-Marc loaned me *Darkness at Noon* by Arthur Koestler, which denounced the evils of communism. Not to be outwitted, Pierre handed me *l'Humanité*, the official communist paper, which he religiously bought every day. "Read it if you really want to know the truth," he exclaimed passionately.

Their prodding at least prompted me to do a lot of reading about the complicated world of politics and to become more informed, although I had to admit that I was a long way from being able to take a position on either side.

At the beginning of October my much-anticipated first day in art school arrived. Early in the morning I rode a bus to the metro terminal in Neuilly and battled the commuter crowd to the Temple station, where I got off a couple of blocks from school. The building was next to a bustling indoor fleamarket *le Carreau du Temple,* a Mecca for inexpensive clothing.

The classrooms were hardly inspiring, with peeling dark green walls, worn stools and work benches splattered with grime and paint. But no matter, I was too excited to care. It would have taken a lot more to dampen my spirits. Besides, the sampling of students' work I'd seen on display demonstrated that a dilapidated interior did not deter creativity. I hoped that one day my work would be there among those chosen few.

During the first semester I went through an orientation in various disciplines. I learned about commercial art, ceramics, sculpture, textiles, interior and industrial design, and spent a couple of weeks in each department. Each department required a student to complete a design project. High marks guaranteed getting a desired major. The most sought-after major was commercial art, which was my first choice. Happily, my project garnered a top grade and a place in that department.

L'Ecole des Arts Appliqués was a three-year all-male art school funded by the city of Paris. It had strict scholastic standards and rigid discipline. To keep my scholarship I needed to maintain high grades. I was determined to do well, and I excelled in most art areas. My work was often held up by professors as an example of originality.

My biggest challenge, however, was getting by on the small monthly allowance Dr. Wexler gave me for carfare and art supplies. Unfortunately I often came up short, because the art supplies cost more than I had. Necessity taught me to become resourceful in cutting corners and learning how to minimize the use of materials. I often rummaged in wastebaskets for discarded tubes and sometimes found tubes still filled with paint.

I met three boys in my commercial art class with whom I eventually formed close friendships. We were quite different from one another, yet we found common ground and admired each other's talent.

There was Lucien Varaut, who wore thick glasses. He was a tall, slender and sensitive boy with delicate hands. Since there was no cafeteria at the school, we brought our own lunches. Lucien and I often ate in the courtyard, munching on our sandwiches while discussing serious topics from art to philosophy.

My sandwich was a piece of baguette with some jam, prepared the night before by Madame Fernande, the jovial cook at the children's home. While the sandwich was tasty enough, it seldom satisfied my hunger. I was left ravenous for most of the day. For his part, my friend had either a Camembert or sardine sandwich that made me salivate with envy.

It began one day as a joke when I said to him with all the earnestness I could muster, "I have read a medical study warning that consuming too much Camembert or sardines is detrimental to artistic creativity." When I saw his startled expression I decided to see how far I could carry on. With a straight face I said, "However, because you are my friend I am willing to sacrifice myself in trading your sandwich for mine whenever you want!" Afterward I told Varaut I was kidding, insisting I'd made up the whole thing. But to no avail; my story had persuaded him that there had to be some truth to the medical claim, and I could not convince him otherwise. Thereafter he insisted I had to share his sandwich, and I happily complied.

My other friend, Edmond Duplan, was a jovial transplanted native of southern France. His distinctive regional accent gave away his origin. He was a bundle of energy, mischievous and happy-go-lucky, always ready with a joke or a funny story. His humor also came through his cartoons, which he dashed off effortlessly on a small pad he carried everywhere. No one, student or professor, was safe from his biting caricatures.

I, too, had a knack for drawing cartoons, and during recess Edmond and I found time to collaborate on a hilarious comic book that we took turns writing and illustrating. I was surprised when Duplan told me that art had not been his first choice; rather, becoming a folk singer had been his lifelong dream. He played the guitar and wrote his own songs, and hoped to be discovered one day.

Finally there was Guy Mandard, with dashing good looks. His thick eyebrows, probing dark eyes and slicked-back jet black hair made quite an impression, especially among the girls. When we occasionally rode the metro together, I was aware of young women casting longing glances at him. Mandard promptly reciprocated with flirtatious winks and smiles. However, for all his playboy demeanor and devil-may-care attitude, he was hardworking and the most talented among my three friends. Whenever we had a design assignment, Mandard's work was invariably among the best, often competing with mine for first place.

Despite my closeness with them, I could not bring myself to confide that I was Jewish or to tell them that I lived in an orphanage. I somehow feared that such a revelation would set us apart. Fortunately for me, my friends seldom alluded to their families, nor did they bother probing into my background. Their curiosity about my private life was never aroused, except once, when on a cold day I arrived at school wearing a red-and-black plaid lumber jacket given to me through an American relief organization. I felt self-conscious wearing it because it stood out like a red flag. Fashion in America obviously was a world apart from French styles. I had quickly made up a story to satisfy my friends' curiosity about the jacket, unwittingly not far from the truth, explaining it was a gift from an uncle living in New York.

My revelation was a hit. Imagine having an American uncle! They couldn't believe that I had never alluded to such an impressive family connection. In the process my lumber jacket suddenly acquired a certain cachet, becoming the height of fashion in their eyes.

Since leaving Cailly-sur-Eure, Alice, Michel and I had kept in touch by writing to each other as often as we could. However, with school vacation not far away, I eagerly counted the days until we would be back together in Paris with Uncle David, Aunt Berthe and

Raoul. While waiting for that much-anticipated event I received a letter from my sister. I was startled to read that the home in Cailly-sur-Eure was closing and that the children would be relocated to other facilities. Alice and Michel were assigned to another home located in Jouy-en-Josas, near Versailles.

The following summer the home in Rueil-Malmaison had to close down, and provisions were made to transfer everybody to another home further from Paris. The news caused much consternation and anguish. I was shattered by the realization that the distance would prevent me from commuting, virtually putting an end to my art studies and dreams. I pleaded with Mrs. Wexler to help me find another place closer to Paris, but to no avail. It seemed hopeless.

Later, while visiting my sister and my brother in Jouy-en-Josas, I spoke about my dilemma with the director of their home, Pierrot Kauffmann, who promised to do his best to help me. As weeks went by my chances looked dimmer, and I was aware that soon I would have to relocate and forget all about my well-laid plans for my future.

At the last minute my reprieve came in the form of a letter from OPEJ, the organization that funded the home in Rueil-Malmaison. Imagine my joy when I read that Pierrot Kauffmann had agreed to take me in, with OPEJ approving my transfer to Jouy-en-Josas.

23

Jouy-en-Josas, Fall 1947

I moved to Jouy-en-Josas just in time to go back to school. The commute was longer and more complicated, with the added challenge of making train and subway connections on time. But it was a small price to pay for the opportunity to go to art school and be reunited with Alice and Michel.

Jouy-en-Josas was a small, picturesque rural town about twenty-five miles southwest of Paris, near Versailles. The children's home consisted of two houses a mile from each other. I was assigned to Les Eglantines, an elegant eighteenth-century mansion, where I joined my sister and about thirty other teenage boys and girls. The other home was named Les Glycines, a smaller residence for younger children, where my brother had been staying.

The children's home was affiliated with the Eclaireurs Israélites de France, a Jewish-French Boy Scout organization. For special occasions everyone wore the navy blue scout uniform. The ambiance at Les Eglantines was friendly, with a strong communal spirit reinforced by Jewish rituals and songs. Mr. Kauffmann usually led the Friday night service, while his wife, nicknamed Feufo, led us in singing Jewish and French folk songs. Mr. Kauffmann, who insisted on being called by his nickname, Pierrot, was in his late twenties, a tall energetic man with dark curly hair and probing eyes. He was quite unpredictable. One moment he was jovial and funny, the next, without warning, cross and moody. Such behavior instilled fear in everybody. But he was liked for his enthusiasm and respected for his leadership.

I'd never heard of the word or concept of Zionism until I met Pierrot. He exhorted all of us to follow his nationalistic ideal by aspiring to settle in Palestine. It was then only a dream that a Jewish state would ever become a reality. Yet Pierrot was confident it could happen. He was a member of a Zionist youth organization called *Hashomer Ha-tzair*, Young Guard, in Hebrew. Its aims, as he explained to us, were to teach Jewish boys and girls scouting techniques and physical preparation for pioneering, with eventual *aliyyah*, immigration to Palestine, as its main goal.

Pierrot's enthusiasm was contagious. Before long he had persuaded most of us that the loftiest goal in our lives ought to be *aliyyah*. I was caught in a dilemma, eager like others to join in, yet held back by my dream of becoming a professional artist.

One day Pierrot told me he needed a special favor from me. I was more than willing to show him my gratitude. I was flattered to hear that he wanted me to paint a mural in the *Hashomer Ha-tzair's* meeting place in Paris. I met him after school in an old warehouse where the reunions took place. He showed me a long wall where the mural was to appear. As Pierrot explained, the overall theme of the mural had to exalt the spirit of pioneering in Palestine.

It was the most ambitious art project I had ever tackled, but I was determined to show Pierrot that his trust in me was justified. On my time off from school I began to outline the mural from sketches Pierrot had approved, filling in the shapes with bold strokes. The theme of Jewish pioneers—men, women and children working in fields, reclaiming Palestine's deserts and transforming them into a green oasis—began to take shape on the wall. The result was more striking than I could ever have expected. It was as though an invisible hand had guided me. I thought it was by far my best work. Nonetheless I felt tense when, weeks later, Pierrot came to inspect the finished mural. To my relief, however, his smiling expression signaled his approval even before he'd uttered a single word.

Pierrot's wife, Feufo, was as spirited as her nickname suggested. The name was an abbreviation of *feu-follet*, meaning firefly. With her lively personality, she brought out the best in everyone by communicating her love for dance and music. She had organized some of the boys and girls into a small chorale and wanted to bring in additional members. I volunteered, knowing that I didn't have a great voice but could carry a tune. I auditioned for Feufo, and she accepted me.

I had to catch up to learn the repertoire of medleys of Hebrew and French folk songs. After the Sabbath service Feufo usually led us in rehearsing the harmonies she'd taught us.

My entry into the chorus couldn't have been more timely. Not long after, Feufo made an exciting announcement: she had arranged to take us on a singing tour of Switzerland during Christmas vacation. We could hardly believe our good fortune, but all the same we wondered if we were ready to face an audience. Feufo was quick to reassure us that with a few more rehearsals we would be just fine.

None of us had traveled abroad before. The prospect of visiting Switzerland became the main topic of conversation, making those who were not members of the chorus envious.

The day finally arrived when we boarded the train at the Gare de Lyon station in Paris proudly wearing our navy blue Scout uniforms. The first stop on our Swiss tour was Basel, which looked like a picture postcard with streets and rooftops buried under a blanket of snow. We were guests at the Jewish community center, where we sang in front of an enthusiastic audience that was apparently unaware of our first-time jitters.

Our next stop was Zurich and another Jewish community center, where we gave several recitals and again were received warmly. Our hosts took us to a lakeside inn for delicious pastries. Our last stop was the mountain ski resort of St. Gallen, near the Austrian border. After one more successful performance we were received by several families who outfitted us with skiing gear and took us to the slopes. For the next couple of days we experienced the heady feeling of gliding on snow, but more often than not we slid on our backsides. Christmas day in St. Gallen couldn't have been a nicer way for me to celebrate my birthday.

Jouy-en-Josas, Spring 1948

Jean Torrès was a friend of Pierrot. He was a familiar sight in Les Eglantines, a man in his late twenties wearing thick glasses that gave him an owlish, absent-minded look. He was a frequent visitor and took an interest in the welfare of the boys and girls of the home and had a kind word for everyone.

I learned that Jean Torrès was a lawyer who had spent the war years in New York, where he had earned his law degree. But the most interesting revelation about him was his connection with the illustrious Jewish statesman Leon Blum. Jean Torrès had become his stepson and lived on the nearby country estate of his famous stepfather. He had been married several times and was currently divorced. He had taken a special interest in my sister, so special that it made me wonder if it was more than friendship. Regardless, it was because of that friendship that my sister, my brother and I were invited by Jean Torrès to an afternoon party at his stepfather's estate.

The gathering was held in a spacious sunroom filled with elegantly dressed guests. The sound of piano music blended with the hum of conversations as waiters unobtrusively wove around the room serving refreshments. Jean Torrès introduced Alice, Michel and me to some of the guests, then led us over to meet his stepfather.

I recognized Leon Blum at once, having seen his picture in the newspapers often. He was a tall, distinguished-looking man with a white mustache, and was talking to another man next to him by the name of Chaim Weizmann. I only wished that my father could have seen me shaking hands with Leon Blum, a man he had often mentioned with reverence and pride. With his strong socialist leanings, my father religiously read *Le Populaire,* a daily newspaper founded by Leon Blum and reflecting his own political views.

Before World War II, from 1936 to 1937, Leon Blum had been prime minister, and was again at the helm of the French government from 1946 to 1947. It was truly astonishing that he, a Jew, had risen to the highest political office in a nation where anti-Semitism was still prevalent.

Among the many guests at the party were important French government officials, including some names I recognized. Others, like Chaim Weizmann, were unknown to me. Jean Torrès later told me about this man, who was a close friend of his stepfather, a famous scientist with an international reputation for important discoveries in chemistry. An English Jew, he was also known for his outspoken support of Zionism and for advocating the formation of a Jewish state in Palestine.

I reflected for days about this memorable party, where I had come into contact with those eminent Jewish leaders. Back in school, feeling elated and proud of these encounters, I wished I could have told the whole story to my friends. But I couldn't muster the courage to reveal my Jewish identity to them.

Alice, Michel and I periodically spent time with Uncle David, Aunt Berthe and Raoul. It always was a joyous occasion when we got together and enjoyed my aunt's delicious lunches and shared the latest happenings in school and in the children's home. My brother showed his excellent report card, garnering approving comments from everyone and earning a couple of francs from our uncle for his piggy bank. I, too, was happy to report that I was doing well in school. As for my sister, who, like myself, had artistic ability, she had successfully completed a photo-retouching course and was about to start a new job in Paris. Not to be left out, Raoul proudly told us he had been accepted to a university for the fall semester.

I was glad to hear Uncle David applaud our efforts. "I hope one day your education will serve you well in America," he said winking at us. Alice and I looked at each other, perplexed, wondering what he meant. My uncle went on to tell us that he was not joking. He had recently been in contact with his mother and brother in New York, who were planning to bring us to the United States. Alice, Michel and I were flabbergasted.

Uncle David carefully explained that he and Aunt Berthe had given a lot of thought to this decision. "We both felt you would have a far better future in America than in France. We love you, but we can't replace your parents." It was the first time he actually intimated that my parents were dead. I suddenly felt numb, and a chill went down my spine. But I was unwilling to accept the inevitable, hoping against hope that a miracle had kept my parents alive. "As your guardian, I took it upon myself to apply for your visas and passports," continued Uncle David.

My sister, my brother and I finally came down to earth. Michel was jubilant at the thought of going to America, but Alice and I didn't know whether to be happy or sad. We both had mixed emotions and needed more time to adjust to the idea. My uncle jokingly said we didn't have to pack yet, because it would take quite a while to get through the slow and complicated French bureaucratic system. On the other side of the Atlantic, more time was needed to locate sponsors willing to pledge our financial support, as was required by the United States.

On the way back to Jouy-en-Josas, Alice, Michel and I talked excitedly about this incredible turn of events. It was difficult to imagine living in the United States and having to learn a new language and different customs. To be sure, the very name "America" conjured in my mind a wealthy and generous country with modern living, fast cars and wide open spaces. But there was also a side, according to books I'd read, of segregation and lynchings.

24

Jouy-en-Josas, Spring 1948
Not long after my uncle's memorable revelation I was dismayed to receive a notice to report for a physical at an army induction center in Paris. Having turned eighteen and being a French citizen, I couldn't possibly avoid the draft. I had to obey the law of the land.

On the specified date I reported to the induction center, a grimy hall filled with bare-chested young men kept in line by arrogant soldiers barking orders. We each waited our turn to appear in front of army doctors for a cursory examination. "Breathe. Exhale. Cough. Next!" That was it. Several weeks later the Department of Defense sent me a notice informing me that I was qualified to serve in the army.

The date of my induction, however, was pending because I was still going to school. The government had been magnanimous enough to allow for a student deferment, giving me a chance to graduate from art school before spending the next two years in the army.

I wondered what my uncle's reaction would be upon hearing that I would be serving in the army, upsetting all the careful plans he'd made to send us to America. Alice said emphatically she would not leave without me. I went at once to see Uncle David and Aunt Berthe to apprise them of my situation. To my great surprise, my uncle reacted quite calmly. "There's no need to get panicky," he said, wisely pointing out that once my student deferment came through, there would be ample time to figure a way out.

On my way back to Jouy-en-Josas I reflected on what my uncle had said, searching for some solution, when suddenly it came to me in a flash. Jean Torrès! He was the answer I'd been seeking. It was no secret that because of his stepfather Jean Torrès had contact with many influential people at the highest levels of the French government. I was hopeful that if he came to my help, he would be able to move mountains with his important connections, yet I realized that it was much too early to celebrate.

Jean Torrès listened to my story carefully and with compassion, and agreed to help me. I knew then that half of the battle had already been won. However, he cautioned me to be patient because, even with important connections, the French bureaucratic wheels moved very slowly. With official affidavits in hand stating that my parents had been deported, Jean Torrès went to work at once.

Some weeks later I met Jean Torrès again, and he looked excited. By his eyes flashing behind his thick lenses and the broad grin on his face I guessed at once that he had succeeded. He then produced an official-looking envelope and carefully extracted the coveted military exemption I'd been seeking, an impressive document bearing fancy seals. I read it through. My name was penned above a lengthy paragraph stating that, because of compelling family hardship, I was discharged from any further military obligations. It was signed by no less than a general of the army and a deputy minister of defense.

Juoy-en-Josas, May 1948

Pierrot, an ardent Zionist, told us with tears of joy about the extraordinary news he'd just heard over the radio: The new nation of Israel was born! For many months before this announcement we'd followed the slow, step-by-step implementation of a plan voted by the United Nations to divide Palestine between Arabs and Jews. At last it was official! Tragically our celebration was short-lived, because the very next day we learned that Israel had been attacked by five Arab nations. We were devastated by press accounts stating that the Israelis were poorly armed and greatly outnumbered. The future for Israel looked grim. Could Israel possibly repel the enemy, we wondered? We dared not contemplate a defeat that would surely end a Jewish homeland before it began.

The war raged for months. Then, slowly and miraculously, the Israelis, on the brink of defeat, turned the tide and pushed the Arab armies back. It was not total victory, but we took comfort from knowing Israel was going to survive.

¶

The year 1948 brought many upheavals in the world, including further separation for Alice, Michel and me. By late spring my sister had elected to move to another home, which had opened exclusively for young working Jewish women, near Versailles. Her move had been inspired by her desire to be more on her own with women of her own age, and at the same time closer to Paris so she could commute to her new job in a photo-retouching studio. Then, during late summer, financial difficulties for the home in Jouy-en-Josas made it necessary to close Les Glycines. All the young children, including my brother, were transferred to another home in Moissac which was affiliated with the Jewish Boy Scouts organization.

Moissac was a small town in southwest France, midway between Bordeaux and Toulouse. By October Les Eglantines was closed for lack of funding. Pierrot had no other choice but to transfer the majority of the boys and girls in his charge to the home in Moissac, while others chose to emigrate to Israel.

I had anxious moments until I learned my fate. To my great relief, Pierrot told us that an interim solution had been found for me and some others who were still going to school in Paris. We would be moved back to Les Glycines, which had been reopened especially for us.

We hardly had settled into the new location when Pierrot tearfully told us that he was stepping down, his stewardship no longer needed in the home because of further cutbacks. His announcement saddened us. His departure seemed to mark the end of an era of camaraderie that he had carefully nurtured during his tenure. I suddenly felt a chill run down my spine, as though the warm spirit of close friendships I had had in the home was already fading away. Pierrot was gone, and with him Alice, Michel and most of my friends, who were now scattered to the four winds.

Jouy-en-Josas, Winter 1949

Jean Martin was a likable young man in his early twenties who had taken over the direction of the home from Pierrot. Despite his closeness to our age, being a medical student gave him a special aura. His responsibility was to handle the home's expenses and give each of us a monthly allowance.

It felt odd being in Les Glycines, where my brother used to live, once filled with noises, cries and laughter of kids playing, and now a house where the only sounds were the hushed conversations of serious-minded young adults. We spent the evenings in the dining room reading or preparing our homework, close to a wood-burning stove to stay warm in the otherwise unheated house.

We had gone through austere times since moving to Les Glycines. Although we were aware of the financial difficulties facing the home, we couldn't help feeling frustrated at times. Food was rationed. Back in Les Eglantines we could always walk into the kitchen and find bread. Here everything was kept under lock and key. Even the cook, the easygoing Madame Costès, complained that she had to spend her own money to buy food for the next meal.

Adding to the growing list of cutbacks, my monthly allowance had shrunk, at a time when school supplies were even more expensive. I wondered to whom I could turn. I was too proud to ask my sister or my uncle for money. Again, by a sheer stroke of luck, Jean Torrès, as ever my savior, recommended me to one of his wealthy friends who was looking for an artist to paint a mural in his apartment in Paris. I was thrilled by the opportunity! My assignment was to copy a reproduction of a painting depicting a pastoral scene into a mural on one of the parlor walls. My new patron was happy with the results, and the generous fee I earned was more than enough to purchase art supplies for the remainder of the school year.

For the past year I'd been following the unfolding saga of Israel, culminating in the defeat of the Arabs and the capture of half of the land the United Nations had planned for a new Arab state. The United Nations tried unsuccessfully to bring the Arabs to the peace table. The Arabs, for their part, refused to recognize the existence of Israel and vowed its destruction.

Later, in January, the first election was held in Israel, and Ben-Gurion was elected prime minister. What caught my attention, however, was the mention that the Israeli parliament had named Chaim Weizmann president. How extraordinary, I thought, recalling Leon Blum's reception, where less than a year before I had met face to face with such an important Jewish leader.

I had just received a letter from two of my friends from Les

Eglantines who recently had made aliyyah to Israel, describing their lives on the *kibbutz* to which they had been assigned. They were living in barracks without any amenities, working in dusty fields under a hot sun with carbines strapped to their backs, to be ready to fight against any sudden attack from Arab marauders. Despite such a harsh existence they were uncomplaining, hopeful that their lives in Israel would soon improve. I had to admire their optimism and grit.

Jouy-en-Josas, Spring 1949

I had promised Michel that I would come to Moissac during Easter vacation to see him, but I couldn't afford to take the bus or the train and hitchhiked instead. I came well prepared with a knapsack, food to last me for a couple of days, a pup tent, a sleeping bag and a compass given to me by Pierrot. One never knew when one's luck would run out. Fortunately many compassionate motorists stopped for me, and I was able to reach Moissac faster than expected, almost in time to celebrate my brother's twelfth birthday.

I could hardly believe seven months had gone by so swiftly since I last saw Michel. The home in Moissac seemed to have agreed with him. He was looking well, taller, and was as impish as ever.

He showed me around and introduced me to his best friend, Bernard, and to Rose and Fanny, two cheerful young women who were in charge of the home for young children of his age. Rose and Fanny told me they were quite fond of my brother, who was a good student and well liked. They were pleased to have met me at last, because Michel often spoke about Alice and me, sharing with them stories about us and eagerly letting them read all our letters.

I spent a wonderful week in Moissac with Michel, enjoying the warm communal spirit of the home, with the Friday night service and singing like it used to be in Les Eglantines. Alas, my vacation was soon over. When I left, Michel broke out in tears. To cheer him up I promised that we would soon be on our way to America, the land of plenty, where candies and chewing gum lined the streets. For my brother, who had a sweet tooth, my humorous and tempting vision was a welcome relief.

To America

25

Versailles, Summer 1949

I graduated from the school of applied art at the end of June by successfully completing all the required courses. The final test for graphic arts was to design a promotional poster and travel brochure for a jazz festival in Harlem, a project that earned me the best grade in my class, my friend Mandard coming a close second. Was it merely a coincidence, or perhaps a good omen, I wondered, that my last design project was all about New York? I felt proud and honored that several of my designs were posted in the school's main hall with other examples of my graduating class's finest work. It seemed like yesterday that I had admired other designs in the same hallway, on my first day of school, wondering if I would ever deserve such recognition.

Over a glass of wine at a local café, my friends Mandard, Duplan, Varaut and I celebrated our graduation, toasting our successful future careers and promising to stay in touch. As I left I wondered if our paths ever would cross again.

Sometime during July, because of ongoing financial difficulties, Les Glycines finally had to close down. This was not entirely unexpected. Jean Martin had complained on many occasions that his budget was stretched to the limit, to which the meager meals Madame Costès improvised could attest. Nonetheless, we were grateful to him for having kept the home open as long as he could and allowing us to finish our school year. It was with some sadness that I said goodbye to Jouy-en-Josas, which held many warm memories for me. Meanwhile Jean Martin had made arrangements to stay with some friends in Paris in order to continue medical school; but as for the rest of us, we were told that we would soon be transferred to the children's home in Moissac.

I was caught on the horns of a dilemma because my uncle had indicated that the time was at hand to finalize our emigration papers, and Alice and I would have to be available to sign some of the documents.

The faraway notion that one day I would emigrate to America suddenly became an urgent reality. If I chose to believe it, I had only to remember Uncle David's prophetic words: "In less then a couple of months you'll be setting foot in America!" I was resigned to going to Moissac, but after discussing the matter with Alice a glimmer of hope for another solution began to take shape.

Still, it was a long shot for my sister to persuade Mrs. Klein, the stern director of her home, to agree to have me until the time of our departure. Would she make an exception in my case and bring a young man into an all-female residence? Mrs. Klein was perhaps not as unyielding as she pretended, or had gotten a favorable impression of me when I had come over to visit Alice. Whatever her reasons were, I was overjoyed to learn from my sister that Mrs. Klein had given her consent.

I moved to the home in Versailles at the end of July. I learned that it had previously been a convent. How ironic, I thought, that young Jewish women would be living in the same place years later. Spanning an entire block, the austere-looking two-story stone structure with tall, narrow windows had the appearance of a school or municipal building. The entry, with massive oak doors, led to a courtyard where I imagined nuns silently shuffling about on the worn cobblestones, prayer books in hand.

Once I had settled in, in order to keep busy and to please Mrs. Klein I offered to paint several murals to liven up the dining hall's drab stone walls, a proposition she readily accepted. After inspecting the finished result, Mrs. Klein, who usually had a pinched look on her face, was all smiles. I felt that I had won her over, and made a friend in the process. Adding to the pleasure I had in painting the murals, many girls of the home came to me and told me how much my bright decorations cheered them up on their way to work.

It took a long time to secure our affidavits, visas and passports, but by late August Alice and I were finally in possession of all the documents we needed to emigrate. At the last minute, however, we discovered that we were not quite ready, because getting money for our passage had suddenly become a major hurdle.

Uncle David, who didn't have the means to help us, had written to his brother Sam in New York and to other relatives there, only to find out that they could not raise the money either. My uncle had then contacted several Jewish agencies in Paris for help, but had been rejected on the grounds that our case was not compelling enough for financial assistance. Many of those organizations were outright skeptical that our American relatives were really unable to fund our trip.

Uncle David said that despite those setbacks he had not yet given up looking for a sponsor. Meanwhile he arranged for Michel to leave Moissac and join Alice and me in Versailles—thanks to Mrs. Klein, who had not objected to taking in another male boarder. My brother's return in the midst of those uncertainties was a balm to our hearts, making us forget our problems and rekindling our optimism.

September came to an end with no solution in sight. Furthermore, while perusing our emigration documents, Alice and I discovered to our dismay that our precious visas were due to expire on October 26, less than a month away. We rushed to see my uncle to inform him of this unexpected wrinkle threatening our emigration, which couldn't have come at a less opportune time. At that juncture the prospect of having to go through another round of bureaucratic tangle in order to renew our visas was quite unsettling. Upon hearing the bad news my uncle threw his hands up in the air. I didn't blame him for being so upset after he had worked so hard to get hold of the documents the first time.

Was it luck or providence, I wondered, that made Uncle David once again contact HIAS, an organization known for providing help to needy Jewish emigrants? The information he gave them about our visas' expiration was apparently what tipped the scales in our favor. Alice, Michel and I were amazed to hear from Uncle David that HIAS had agreed to pay for our passage.

However, while one crisis was averted another problem had emerged. We had to locate a ship sailing to America in time. It seemed that once more we were locked in a race against the clock. As our hopes dwindled, at the last minute HIAS miraculously located and booked us on the S.S. *Sobiesky*, a tourist ship coming from Italy bound for the United States. By chance the *Sobiesky* was scheduled to make a brief off-shore stop in Cannes to pick up mail on October 3, and to arrive in New York on October 25, exactly twenty-four hours before our visas would expire.

Suddenly we had only a couple of days left to pack and say goodbye to our close friends. Aunt Berthe treated us to a delicious farewell dinner, during which she dispensed some last minute advice about traveling. Upon hearing that Alice was going to carry money she'd saved at work, my aunt cautioned her to be careful, especially on a ship with so many strangers. She told my sister about a foolproof way to avoid losing her money or having it stolen, by sewing the bills into her girdle, a trick she had learned many years ago from an aunt in Poland when she immigrated to France.

With a broad smile Uncle David said that he and Aunt Berthe wanted to give us a special going-away present, something useful that would always remind us of them. Then, like a magician, he deftly extracted from one of his coat pockets three beautiful watches ticking in unison. Alice, Michel and I were left speechless, lost in admiration of such princely gifts.

We took an overnight train to Cannes, the famous seaside resort on the French Riviera. Uncle David, Aunt Berthe and Raoul came to see us off at the Gare de Lyon in Paris. After tearful goodbyes we staked claim to three seats in a compartment and stowed our luggage on the overhead rack. Alice heaved a sigh of relief, happy that we finally were on our way, still clutching the pocketbook in which she kept our precious documents safely fastened with safety pins.

From my window I had a last fleeting vision of the Paris suburbs quickly fading under darkening skies. The next morning we were greeted in Cannes by radiant sunshine and a cloudless blue sky. After checking into an expensive hotel with vouchers given to us by HIAS, we had an entire day at our disposal to pretend we were tourists.

The view along the promenade was breathtaking, with palm

trees and posh hotels overlooking the blue expanse of the Mediterranean Sea. Even though it was late October the beach was dotted with red-and-white parasols and vacationers taking advantage of the balmy weather. We were scheduled to board the ship the next day, which left us some extra time to visit the town and stroll around the harbor, which was filled with sailboats and expensive-looking yachts.

In the evening we reported to the customs house in the harbor, where an agent inspected our suitcases and stamped our passports. There we followed several postmen into a motor launch loaded with large canvas mailbags. As the launch leaped noisily across the waves toward the ship, the coastline quickly melted into the night. Only the flickering light of a lighthouse was visible on the shore, blinking a last *adieu*.

The *Sobiesky* emerged from the darkness with hundreds of bright lights outlining the decks above us. We gingerly climbed to the top along a precarious-looking metal stairway hugging the towering black hull. A steward led us to our sleeping quarters, a steerage compartment in the bowels of the ship. There we were assigned to bunks in a dormitory filled with dozens of other passengers already asleep and snoring, other penurious emigrants like us who could not afford better accommodations. But we were not about to complain, since we would be allowed to take our meals and use the ship's facilities like tourist-class passengers.

After crossing the Strait of Gibraltar, the *Sobiesky* steadfastly plowed the steel-gray waves of the Atlantic ocean, day after day getting ever closer to the new world. Fortunately it was an uneventful crossing except for our occasional bouts of seasickness. For twelve days Alice, Michel and I were at sea, held captive by the endless vastness of the ocean, unfurling wave after wave around us, with only the horizon in sight.

On our thirteenth day, the last day of our crossing, seagulls appeared circling over the ship, a sure sign that land was near. The thick morning fog over the water began to dissipate, offering us our first look at faraway skyscrapers rising over the horizon. Alice, Michel and I joined the other passengers on deck, anxious to have our first sight of New York. Taken in tow by a red tugboat that spewed dense black smoke, our ship slowly inched its way toward the harbor. Excited cries and shouts suddenly erupted when some passengers spied the silhouette of the Statue of Liberty in the distance. Unfortunately it was too crowded on deck for us to see the famous icon of freedom that we'd heard so much about.

The gray shroud hovering over the bay lifted slowly, bringing into sharp focus other large ships and ferryboats crisscrossing the harbor. Every minute brought us closer to the forest of skyscrapers that lined the shore like giant sentries guarding New York. The *Sobiesky* glided silently alongside a pier next to long gray hangars and finally came to a full stop, the muffled sounds of engines slowly dying away.

On the pier below, forklifts with burly-looking longshoremen wearing heavy winter jackets were already assembled, ready to unload the ship. As I leaned over the railing and looked at those strong men, it occurred to me that not too long ago those same men might have been the G.I.s who journeyed to France to liberate us from the terror of the Nazi occupation. I felt tears of gratitude running down my cheeks, for I felt that I owed them my freedom.

I wished that my impressions would remain intact in my mind forever. That was the day when my sister, my brother and I stepped down onto a New York pier, our first steps on American territory. Steps that would forever change our destinies.

Epilogue

Half a century has elapsed since Alice, Michel and I stepped onto that pier in Manhattan. Our first few years in the United States were not happy ones. We struggled economically and felt the frustration of having to learn a new language and assimilate a new culture. We soon discovered that my grandmother and uncle were worlds apart from the popular French notion that Americans lived in the lap of luxury. Actually I had not entertained such an idea, but I had not been prepared to find that they were barely above poverty level; Grandmother Tessie lived on Social Security in a small, dark, dingy-looking apartment on Second Avenue on the lower east side of Manhattan.

As for Uncle Sam and his family, they were hardly better off in a cramped two-bedroom railroad flat on Cortelyou Road off Ocean Parkway in Brooklyn. Their apartment was already crowded before Alice, Michel and I moved in with them, with my uncle, his wife by a second marriage, her children, a grown-up son, a married daughter, her husband and their two young boys.

I couldn't blame them for feeling quite unhappy about our intrusion. Not knowing the language also contributed to friction and misunderstanding. No one told us why Uncle Sam had taken us in. My guess was that, as our closest relative in the U.S., he felt obligated to help us, probably compelled by the tragic events of the Holocaust that had destroyed most of his family in Europe. Nonetheless it must have been difficult convincing his wife to let more people live with them, especially since my aunt and her children had no prior family or emotional ties to us.

My uncle was in his mid-sixties when we arrived, but he looked older because of tuberculosis he had contracted while working as a house painter. He had recovered from this terrible disease but had little physical strength. He was retired, living on a small pension and contributions from his family. He was soft-spoken and gentle, often smiling with a twinkle in his pale gray eyes that lighted his lined but still handsome face.

When we came to America there was a recession, and jobs were scarce. Yet my sister managed to get a well-paying job in photo-retouching in Manhattan. As for me, without actual training in commercial art and unable to speak English, I was grateful to find a job as a messenger for an advertising agency.

Alice and I gave our entire pay to my aunt and only kept enough for carfare. Michel was enrolled in the neighborhood public school and made quick progress in English, faster than mine, I must admit! About six months later I found another job, working for a famous French poster designer named Jean Carlu. It was actually my first job in the art field, and as his assistant I learned a great deal by observing one of the top designers of that era.

When I spoke English well enough to be understood and even to express humor, it was as though a curtain had been lifted, allowing me to face the future optimistically.

Despite the fact that I was not yet a citizen, I was drafted and inducted into the United States Army in May 1951. After my basic training in Fort Lee, Virginia, I was shipped to Japan, then to Korea, assigned to an infantry unit on the front line with the Fifth Regimental Combat Team, dug in on top of a frozen hill. For the next sixteen months I slept in a bunker, ate C-rations and tried to stay alive while artillery rounds rained upon my outfit as we fought back Chinese troops determined to overrun our lines. But my luck held out, and I survived the grim terror of combat. In March 1953 I was discharged from the army and returned to civilian life.

When I came back to Brooklyn I was fortunate to find a job as a package designer, working for Equitable, a company manufacturing paper bags in Long Island City. I had no experience in such a specialized field but quickly learned the ropes. Since I was able to provide for myself I left my uncle, taking Michel along, and moved to a one-room basement apartment nearby. With the little money my brother saved working after school in a neighborhood grocery, and with my army mustering-out pay, I was able to buy a piece of the American dream: a used car!

Alice had moved out to Rochester while I was in Korea, having found a job with Kodak. For her it was a golden opportunity to leave the confinement of my uncle's apartment, becoming independent in the process. She wrote to us and managed to come down to Brooklyn to see us from time to time.

And so, after trying beginnings, once we became financially independent the three of us led lives free of the turmoil of the past. We married, had children and even grandchildren. We were able to find freedom, prosperity and even happiness in our adoptive land, our sweet revenge for Hitler's monstrous design to erase the entire Jewish people from the face of the earth.

About My Immediate Family

I am fortunate that everyone in my immediate family is alive and well. My sister, brother and I are still very close, except that distance keeps us apart. Nonetheless, our families get together for holidays and other occasions, and we are only a phone call away.

Alice and her husband, Sidney Goldman, live in Baldwin, New York, and are both retired now. Incidentally, I was responsible for introducing my sister to Sidney, whom I'd met in the army. They have two grown children, Eli and Stephanie, and from their daughter two grandchildren, Sonya and Benjamin.

Michel and his wife, Joan, live in Paoli, Pennsylvania. They have two grown boys, Claude and Kenny. Michel went on to become an electrical engineer. He earned his doctorate and is now employed with Lockheed Martin as a noted expert in aerospace and satellite communications. He has written several technical books and has also lectured internationally.

My wife, Cécile (née Rojer), and I make our home in Pomona, near New York City. She came from Belgium and was also a hidden child during the war. Her parents were deported in 1943 and died in Auschwitz. Cécile immigrated to the U.S. during the late forties with her older sister, Anny, and her younger brother, Charly, who also managed to survive. Cécile's charm, individuality, humor and optimism were hard to resist. I fell in love with her. We were married on November 6, 1955. For a while Cécile taught ballroom dancing, then did office work until we had children.

Eventually we were blessed with two wonderful and talented daughters, Aviva and Linda, and five grandchildren. Aviva, the eldest, is a successful trial lawyer who also finds time to teach aerobics part-time and run marathons. She lives in Boston with her husband, Michael Abrahams, and their three children: Talia, thirteen; Danny, eleven; and Adam, nine.

Linda, a professional mother like her sister, is presently general manager and the managing partner of Deutsch, a New York advertising agency. She and her husband, Jon Sawyer, and their two children, Sam, nine, and his brother, Bryce, four, live outside of New York City, in Larchmont nearby.

Since retiring a couple of years ago, I found more time to indulge in pursuits my busy working schedule had not allowed me in the past. Writing this book, for instance, was a novel and wonderful challenge to my mind, as well as cathartic. I also found more time to paint, sketch and try other artistic endeavors. I also now have the luxury to play tennis as often as I wish, a sport I love and which keeps me fit. Fitness also plays an important part in Cécile's life. With her dancing background she went on to teach aerobics, a rewarding part-time career that still continues.

I began my career as a package designer strictly by accident, because a good job offer had come my way. That first step led me to other jobs in the same field, gaining valuable experience in each one as I was promoted to higher positions: at an art studio in Manhatten, then at Colgate-Palmolive, and finally with the cosmetic firm Revlon, where I spent three years as director of packaging and design.

With the experience gained in Revlon I left to become a freelance designer specializing in cosmetic and fragrance designs. I soon met with success and was able to establish a good reputation among many large corporations specializing in beauty products. In addition to my packaging design work I diversified into other areas of art. I always was fascinated by graphic design and found a rewarding outlet in designing book jackets and illustrating children's books for leading publishers.

About My Extended Family

Alas, time inevitably exacts its toll. Sickness and old age took all my relatives away. Uncle Sam, who was in fragile health, died in the late fifties. Grandmother Tessie predeceased her son, stricken by a heart attack in 1953, shortly after I was discharged from the army. I was glad that I got to know them at least briefly, even though the language barrier prevented any real intimacy between us.

Nonetheless I have kept warm memories of the weekly visits Michel and I paid to our grandmother, with each visit following the same ritual. She looked so happy to see us, her eyes shining behind her rimless glasses. She always had a scrubbed look, her smooth face almost wrinkle-free and her snowy white hair neatly combed. She was overweight, but surprisingly nimble as she trotted around her apartment.

We went food shopping for my grandmother along First Avenue, often mistaking what she wanted despite our best efforts to figure out her own concoction of English and Yiddish. She invariably prepared a lamb stew for us, which she kept simmering in a pot for hours. Nonetheless Michel and I managed to fake our enthusiasm to please her. Grandmother Tessie subscribed to the *Forward* newspaper's Yiddish edition. As a result the apartment was crowded with musty, yellowing piles of newspapers. She loved them so much that she couldn't bear to throw them out.

Uncle David, Aunt Berthe and Cousin Raoul are no longer alive. Only one year after I took my first trip back to France in 1967 with my wife and children and spent a couple days with them, Aunt Berthe died in her sleep from a heart attack. Raoul, who had a successful career for many years with Chrysler as a top marketing executive, contracted a lingering illness and died prematurely in the early seventies. By then Uncle David had developed a lucrative clientele and moved to a nicer apartment in Paris.

Uncle David survived Aunt Berthe by about ten years and died of cancer in the late seventies. During that period of time he came to visit my family in America a number of times. During those occasional visits my daughters grew quite fond of him, with his gentle demeanor and impish grin. Questions about the past always came up, of course. My sister had the presence of mind to tape a conversation with him on a host of subjects dealing with family history. I even asked him what had caused the rift between him and my mother. He seemed embarrassed to tell me. Actually, it turned out to be a silly fight that forever changed the course of their relationship.

When Uncle David and Aunt Berthe immigrated to France they remained for a while with my parents until they could find a place of their own. He remembered how tiny the apartment was and how easy it was to get on each other's nerves, especially for my mother and Berthe, who didn't get along. He reminded me that they all were young people in their early twenties. One day my mother went shopping with Alice, who was then only an infant, and had asked Uncle David to keep an eye on the food cooking on the stove. He simply forgot, and the dinner was burned. My mother was irate and yelled at him and Aunt Berthe. A terrible fight ensued, and the same day my uncle and aunt packed up and left, never to see them again.

That was the whole story! I could not believe they were not able to patch up their differences; unfortunately Aunt Berthe and my mother, who wanted their own way, had stood in the way of any possible reconciliation. Well, I thought, my uncle and aunt had certainly redeemed themselves. Sadly, a tragedy was needed to bring out the best in them.

From the few members of my family who survived the Holocaust, I certainly would be remiss if I didn't mention that completely out of the blue, during the middle of the seventies, I was contacted by a cousin on my father's side who had escaped the clutches of the Nazis. This cousin, named Reuven, his father, Jacob (one of my father's brothers), and his wife, Yeda, were the only ones from their entire family who managed to flee from Poland. They made their way to Russia, where they remained until the end of the war. Jacob died there of natural causes. Later Reuven and his mother settled in Israel.

Through the Yad Vashem Holocaust research center in Jerusalem Reuven found out that Alice, Michel and I were still alive; and so, after a great deal of investigating, he finally tracked us down.

After Reuven contacted me we began an active correspondence. He later came to see us while on a business trip for El Al.

Thus we continued our relationship, capping it with a trip to Israel in the late seventies, when we met his wife, children and mother. My Aunt Yeda recalled the times when my parents came to Poland on a visit with Alice and me: "You were about two years old and quite a little devil," she said. Afterwards time eroded our contacts. We eventually lost touch with one another, perhaps due to our lack of common interests or because of the great differences in our cultural backgrounds.

About My Parents and Their Close Friends

Joseph Krum, who was hidden with me in St. Aubin-les-Elbeuf, survived the war and went on to have a successful career managing a large department store in Paris. He was married and had two children. The war had left deep scars on him, however, from which he never recovered. After several nervous breakdowns he eventually took his life in the late eighties. Cécile and I have remained friends with his wife, Malvina.

Joseph's parents died in Auschwitz in the summer of 1942, shortly after they were arrested with my parents. I found their names listed in a book by Serge Klarsfeld, the well-known Nazi hunter. Using meticulous records kept by the Nazis during the war, he was able to compile a list of Jews from France who were deported and who perished in concentration camps.

It would seem logical, then, that my parents, who were arrested together with their friends would have met the same fate, and as such their names should be found alongside those of their friends in the Nazi files. But there is nothing of the sort, as though my father and mother simply vanished into thin air.

During the early nineties, right after the collapse of communism, access was opened to many files pertaining to victims of the Holocaust in countries such as East Germany and Russia, where until that time they had been sealed from the public. This renewed my hope that I might get a fresh lead on my parents. At that time I began a thorough inquiry, writing to every Holocaust related organization in the U.S., France, and Israel that might shed some light on their fate.

I even contacted the International Red Cross. To this day, however, my parents' names have never appeared anywhere.

At times during my dogged search I wondered why I was so driven to find the answer to their disappearing. Nothing would change, even if I was able to uncover the truth. I came to the conclusion that it was my own way of mourning for them, a process I never was able to do consciously. I hoped that knowing where they died would lift the pain and anxiety I felt and give me the sense of peace and closure for which I'd been searching for many years.

About the People I Met During the War

Regrettably, I never saw Mr. and Mrs. Bonneau again, although I kept in touch with their daughter, Madeleine, and her husband. In the early eighties they came to the U.S. and spent a couple of days with us, during which time we had a chance to reminisce about Madeleine's parents, who by then had passed away. Time eventually eroded my correspondence with Madeleine, and we gradually lost contact.

On the other hand, Alice, Cécile and I are still in touch with the Ledauphin family. During our many trips to France, when Cécile and I went to see them, Madeleine's spirits never waned, despite her deep personal losses. First her husband died in the fifties then in the sixties cancer took her daughter, Solange.

For many years Madeleine's son, Wilfrid, married with two children, owned a lucrative photography store in St. Hilaire du Harcouet, a town badly destroyed by American bombers in 1944 during the liberation. The main square where the store is located was reduced to rubble, but it was rebuilt exactly as it was before the war. Madeleine sold her farm and moved to a house a couple blocks away from her son. Few farms in Savigny-le-Vieux have remained. Most of them were sold and renovated as summer homes for Parisians wanting rustic country retreats. In the past year Madeleine was no longer able to look after herself and had to be put in a nursing home.

Every time I went to see the Ledauphins I took the opportunity to look up the places in Savigny-le-Vieux where I had been hidden and the people who sheltered me. On my first visit, many years ago,

I learned that Mrs. Prim and le Père Geslin had passed away. Mère Geslin was still alive, however. Later on, Roland and Thérèse ran the farm until they both retired. Then Thérèse's children took over.

During my last visit a couple of years ago the farmhouse was still pretty much the same on the outside, except for the thatched roof which had been replaced with slate. The dirt lane leading to the farm had become a ribbon of asphalt, and parked in front, instead of old rusty bicycles and horse carts, were two late-model cars. The twentieth-century had finally caught up with this rural area. Even the interior of the house had been modernized with electricity, running water, a gleaming ceramic tile floor, a refrigerator and a television and VCR set in a prominent place. Next door, Mrs. Prim's house had undergone similar improvements. The countryside and the village remained unchanged, although the village looked deserted. I looked up Mr. Crochet, the teacher who generously gave me paper, paint and books, who was still hale and alert. He had even saved all the drawings I had given him. We reminisced about the past and about the old-timers who, for the most part, had passed on. What about Mrs. Huard, I inquired? No one seemed to know what had happened to her or her daughter.

Incidentally, Annette, the little girl hidden with her brother and me, traced me back through Mr. Crochet and then through the Ledauphins, who had my address. We were reunited several years ago in Limoges, where she lives with her husband. Annette was still haunted by memories of the war. We compared notes on what we each remembered of those grim years. More recently Cécile and I got together again with Annette and her husband and made another pilgrimage to Savigny-le-Vieux, rekindling the past. On another trip we visited the nearby site of the landing and the cemetery of Omaha Beach, paying homage to the G.I.s who gave their lives for us.

In the early 1990s, my brother, while vacationing with his wife in Normandy, renewed contact with Gaston Leclère for the first time since the war. By then his parents were already deceased. Their emotional reunion prompted Gaston and his family to take a trip to the U.S., during which they alternately stayed with my brother, my sister and me. I had an opportunity to ask him about the past, and I was surprised to learn that his father and Mr. Ernst had been involved with the local French partisans, even as they went about their regular jobs, risking their lives in the process.

I also learned that Mr. Ernst's black market activities got him into trouble shortly after Joseph and I left. He was arrested and sent to a German labor camp and released at the end of the war. Afterwards he moved to Rouen, a nearby industrial city, where he settled and prospered as a successful textile broker. I was disappointed that Gaston could not shed much light on Mr. Ernst's relationship with the Bonneaus. However, he remembered that his parents had received some money for Michel's upkeep through Mr. Ernst, but only for two or three months, after which Mr. Ernst claimed that the Bonneaus stopped paying him. Nonetheless, Gaston's parents, who had grown fond of my brother, decided they would shoulder the expense of looking after him.

Sadly I learned that Gaston died the following year after a brief illness. Since that time his wife, Micheline, her children and grandchildren have remained in touch with us, and her granddaughter divided her summer vacation between visits to my brother, my sister and me.

I have not kept many contacts from the children's homes. But I did keep track of my friends Sami and Michel from Cailly-sur-Eure for a while. In 1947 they attempted to reach Israel by ship, only to be stopped by the British navy and interned in a prison camp on the island of Cyprus for almost a year. After their release they both fought in the Israel War of Independence, Michel losing an eye from an exploding shell. Years later, however, Sami was still unable to adapt to the life there and went back to France with his wife and children and settled near Paris.

Through the media I was reminded of the Cohn-Bendits, who were in charge of the children's home. Their youngest son, Daniel, who was only an infant when I was in Cailly-sur-Eure, achieved international notoriety during the latter part of the 1960s. Known as "Danny the Red" (I remember his flaming red hair) Daniel Cohn-Bendit led the largest-ever student protest in Paris for grievances against the French government. When police tried to squash the protest, demonstrations erupted in other cities. Soon all of France had come to a standstill as workers went on strike to demonstrate their solidarity against the government. Inspired and emboldened by Danny the Red's example, students from other countries also marched to demand reforms from their governments.

Not too long ago I received a letter with a listing of names of children who were in Jouy-en-Josas. Many now live in Israel, others in France. I got in touch with some of them. I was happy to find out that the director of the home, Pierrot, was alive and well, still involved with Jewish organizations in Paris. Sadly, his wife Feufo died a few years ago. Jean Torrès married one of the girls from the home and has remained committed to helping needy Jewish children. On my last trip to France I went to Jouy-en-Josas to have one last look at Les Eglantines. This eighteenth-century château was even more beautiful than I remembered it, and had been refurbished as a museum for regional arts and crafts.

On one of my recent trips to Paris I went to see l'Ecole des Arts Appliqués, my old art school. I was surprised to find that the exterior stone-and-brick facade had been cleaned and restored to its original condition, revealing a rather handsome building, not the drab structure I remembered. I went inside with the permission of the concierge. The hallway downstairs had student artwork posted along the walls—rather disappointing examples, viewed from my perspective as a professional artist. It made me wonder if my work there had been of the same caliber, better or worse.

The school had become coed and a four-year college. A wind of freedom of expression had obviously swept through the staid art school I attended more than fifty years ago. Students were going to classes nonchalantly wearing torn jeans, outrageous T-shirts, punk hair styles and nose rings, listening to radios and smoking. I heaved a sigh of relief when I noticed that the classrooms were still the same, with easels and stools piled up in the corners and paint-splattered desks. The visit reminded me of the longtime relationships I've maintained with my three friends from art school. Since those days when I shared sandwiches with Lucien Varaut, drew cartoons with Edmond Duplan and competed for first place with Guy Mandard, I have remained in close contact with them.

About two years ago I visited Mandard, with whom I had kept the closest ties. To celebrate my visit he had organized a surprise reunion of our close school friends and also of some other "old-timers" from the School of Applied Arts. Unfortunately Varaut had died a couple of years before. It was quite a special occasion to be together with our wives, having a great time and comparing notes about our youthful school dreams and what paths we eventually followed.

Duplan was never happy in the art field. In mid-career he returned to his native village near the Pyrénées and fulfilled his childhood dream of becoming a folksinger, playing the guitar and writing his own songs. Since then his concerts have taken him around southern France, where he has become somewhat of a celebrity. As for Mandard, some time ago he too gave up a fairly successful advertising and design business to become a full-time painter and sculptor. He is quite talented and has frequent shows in Paris. Over the years Cécile and I have stayed many times with the Mandards, and reciprocated when they have come on vacation to the U.S.

About Some of My Parent's Business Friends

Some of my parents' business friends who were also Polish Jews managed to survive the horrors of the war. Among them are Mr. and Mrs. Eichenbaum and their three children. (Mr. Eichenbaum was instrumental in helping my father to emigrate to France from Poland by offering him a job. It was in his house in Vincennes that my parents were married.) It seemed that about one year before France went to war, Mr. Eichenbaum's once-thriving watch business came upon hard times, and eventually he was bankrupted. Rather than face his creditors Mr. Eichenbaum fled to the U.S., where he had connections. Later he obtained visas for his family, who left France in 1940, practically on the last ship sailing for America. It is rather ironic that his financial difficulties saved him and his family. There is little doubt that, had he continued to do well, he would have remained in France and met my parents' fate. During the late fifties I located the Eichenbaums in Brooklyn. They had changed their name to the more English-sounding Ashley. I kept in touch with them for a while, but eventually lost contact.

Mr. Friedman was another business friend of my father who also managed to escape with his wife and children the clutches of the Nazis. His wife later committed suicide, however, unable to resume a normal life. It is sad that some people fortunate enough to have survived through the horrific conditions were so traumatized that they no longer found life worth living.

I often think that in exchange for all the tragedies I encountered in my youth I've been given an extra dose of optimism, hope and an appreciation for life, for all it has to offer.

Postscript

Pomona, October 2000

Amazingly, just on the eve of my departure for a "Jewish Heritage Tour" of Eastern Europe, which is to include a visit to Auschwitz, I finally learned my parents' fate, and a mystery that has haunted me for so many years has suddenly come to an end. Even though for years I fervently hoped to find an explanation for their disappearance, the information and evidence that my mother and father were deported to Auschwitz brings a painful re-awakening of tragic memories.

The information I have received comes from Serge Klarsfeld, the noted French Nazi-hunter and Jewish activist, with whom I have corresponded in the past, hoping that he would be able to help me in my search. He is the author of *Mémorial de la Déportation des Juifs de France*, compiled from retrieved Nazi files and published in 1978. My parents' name is not to be found in that voluminous book, which lists about seventy thousand names of Jewish men, women, and children who perished in Auschwitz.

However, only a short time ago, Klarsfeld solved this mystery. After carefully cross-checking my parents' birthdates, birthplaces, and surnames against those listed in his book, he spotted matching data listed next to the surname Zernebin, once with my mother's first name, Syma (she called herself Sonia in France), and again with my father's name, Wolf (called Samuel in France). Zernebin has a faint resemblance to Jeruchim; yet there is no doubt that every other bit of information given for the "Zernebins" matches my parents exactly.

Klarsfeld explained that he had found written documentation of my parents' arrest as they attempted to cross into the non-occupied zone of France, and this evidence corroborated his findings. He sent

239

me copies of two handwritten cards, most likely recorded by the French police, listing accurately my parents' birthdates and birthplaces, nationality, and home address in Montreuil. It all matched except for the strange last name. How could this be accounted for? Klarsfeld surmised that my parents carried false identity papers at the time of their arrest, and when they were asked by the police for their real name, their foreign accent led to this confused spelling of Jeruchim.

Also written on the cards is "Poitiers," the name of the town or vicinity where my parents were arrested, and the date of their arrest is given as September 11, 1942.

Klarsfeld also sent me a copy of a document tracing my parents' whereabouts from the time of their arrest to their incarceration in the camp at Drancy. This official letter pertained to them and to other unfortunate Jews who had also attempted to escape to the non-occupied zone. This memorandum, written on September 12, 1942, by Jean Leguay, a high-ranking member of the National French Police, was sent to the Gestapo chief in Paris, one Obersturmführer Rotke, informing him that Jews rounded up in the non-occupied zone would be transferred to Nazi authorities, and stated with chilling detail that a convoy of 600 to 650 Jews of foreign origin would be crossing the line of demarcation at Vierzon on September 15, 1942, at 1:51 P.M. They were to depart Vierzon the same day at 2:40 P.M. and arrive at Bourget-Drancy that night at 10:23.

And so the mystery of my parents' disappearance has finally been solved, at the dawn of a new millennium, fifty-nine years after they were murdered by the Nazis. As I prepare myself to honor their memories by stepping on the bitter soil of Poland, near the site where, in the prime of their lives, my parents were herded and sent to the gas chambers, I will say goodbye to them and to all the other innocent victims of the Holocaust.

Time has not succeeded in erasing the pain of the loss of my parents. I will always miss them and grieve for them. Yet I hope that this pilgrimage will give me some comfort and the courage to cast away the lingering shadows of a cruel and distant past.